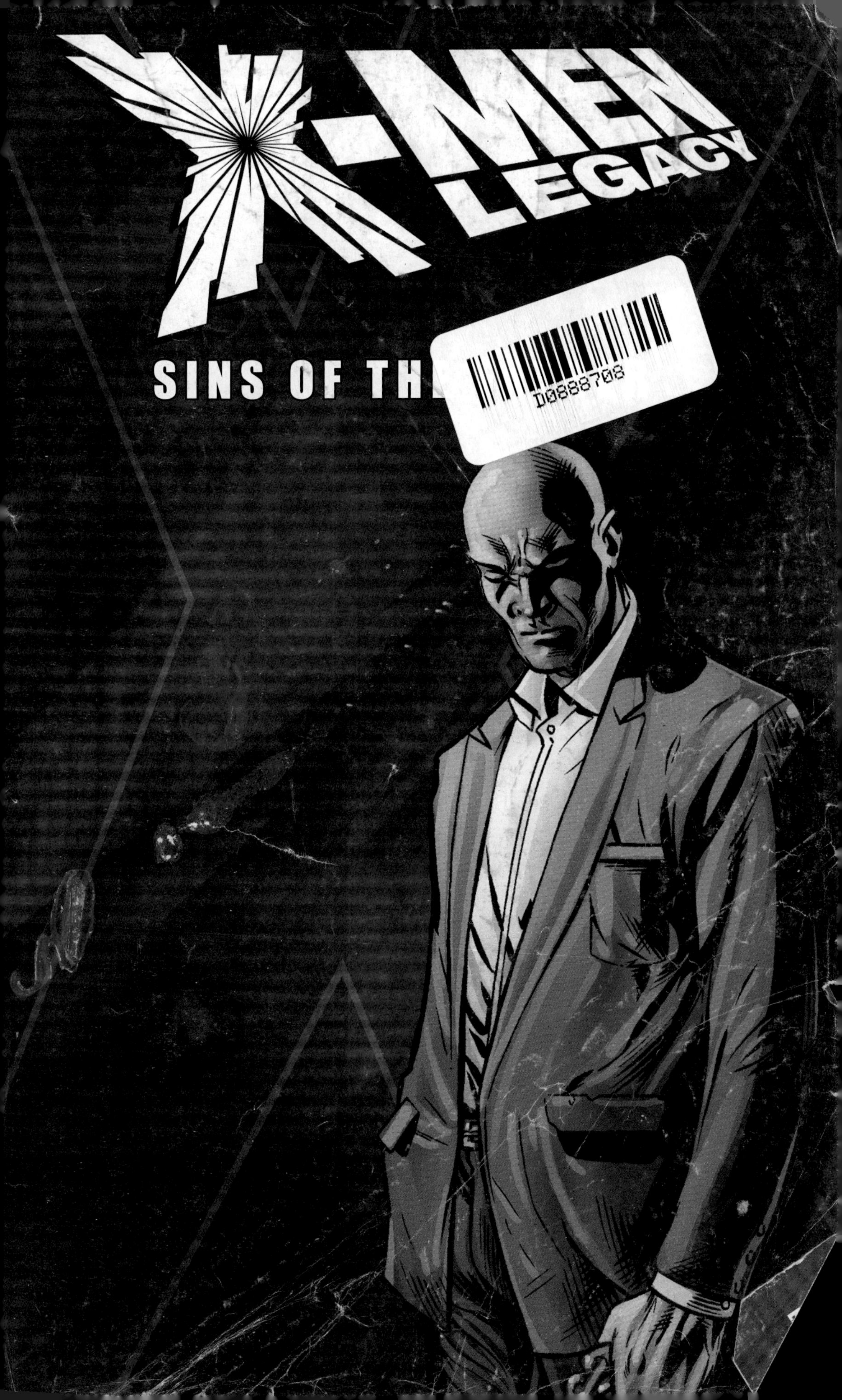
X-MEN
LEGACY
SINS OF THE
D0888708

X-MEN LEGACY

SINS OF THE FATHER

WRITER: Mike Carey

ISSUE #213:
PENCILER: Scot Eaton
INKER: Drew Hennessey
COLORIST: Frank D'Armata

ISSUE #214:
PENCILER: Scot Eaton
INKER: Drew Hennessey
COLORIST: Frank D'Armata
MINDSCAPE SEQUENCES:
PENCILER: Ken Lashley
INKER: Paul Neary
COLORIST: Edgar Delgado

ISSUE #215:
PENCILER: Scot Eaton
INKER: Drew Hennessey
COLORIST: Frank D'Armata
ROGUE AND HELLFIRE SEQUENCES:
ARTIST: Marco Checchetto
COLORIST: Jean-Francois Beaulieu

ISSUE #216:
PENCILER: Phil Briones
INKER: Scott Hanna
COLORIST: Brian Reber

LETTERER: Cory Petit
COVER ART: Alan Davis, Ken Lashley & Salvador Larroca
ASSISTANT EDITORS: Will Panzo & Daniel Ketchum
EDITOR: Nick Lowe
EXECUTIVE EDITOR: Axel Alonso

X-MEN: ODD MEN OUT ONE-SHOT

"ODD MEN OUT"
WRITER: Roger Stern
PENCILER: Dave Cockrum
INKER: Joe Rubinstein
COLORIST: Andrew Crossley
LETTERER: Dave Sharpe

"THE NEW MUTANTS THINK AGAIN"
WRITER: Mike Higgins
PENCILER: Dave Cockrum
INKER: Joe Rubinstein
COLORIST: Andrew Crossley
LETTERER: Joe Rosen

COVER ART: Eric Nguyen
ASSISTANT EDITOR: Suzanne Gaffney
EDITOR: Bob Harras

X-MEN: THE UNLIKELY SAGA OF XAVIER, MAGNETO & STAN
WRITER: Stan Lee
PENCILERS: Ron Lim, Ben Oliver, Ron Frenz, Klaus Janson, Sean Chen, John Romita Jr., Pasqual Ferry, Leinil Francis Yu & Howard Chaykin
INKERS: Mostafa Moussa, Ben Oliver, Tom Palmer, Klaus Janson, Sandu Florea, Scott Hanna, Pasqual Ferry, Leinil Francis Yu & Howard Chaykin
COLORIST: Guru eFX
LETTERER: Virtual Calligraphy's Joe Caramagna
COVER: Brandon Peterson
ASSOCIATE EDITORS: John Barber & Nicole Boose
EDITOR: Ralph Macchio

COLLECTION EDITOR: Jennifer Grünwald
EDITORIAL ASSISTANT: Alex Starbuck
ASSISTANT EDITORS: Cory Levine & John Denning
EDITOR, SPECIAL PROJECTS: Mark D. Beazley
SENIOR EDITOR, SPECIAL PROJECTS: Jeff Youngquist
SENIOR VICE PRESIDENT OF SALES: David Gabriel
PRODUCTION: Jerry Kalinowski
BOOK DESIGNER: Spring Hoteling

EDITOR IN CHIEF: Joe Quesada
PUBLISHER: Dan Buckley

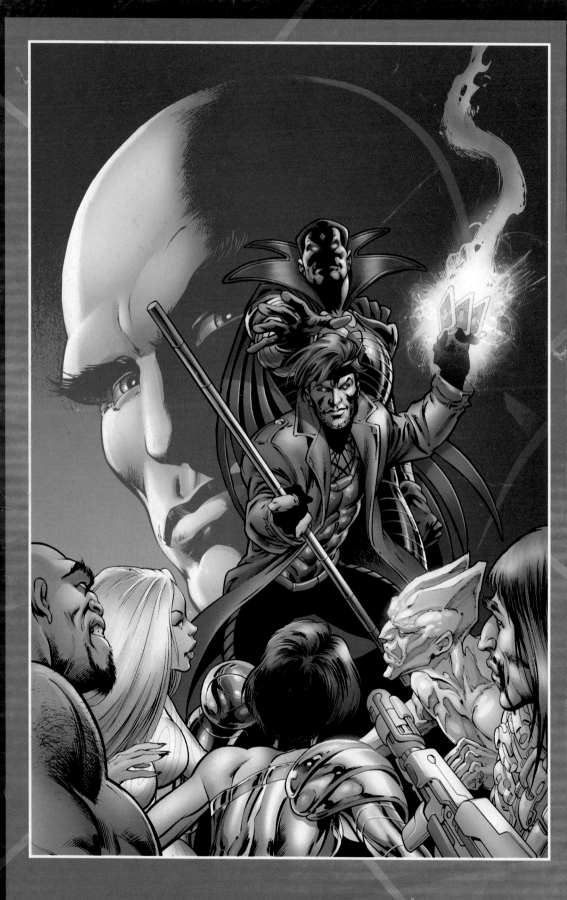

#213

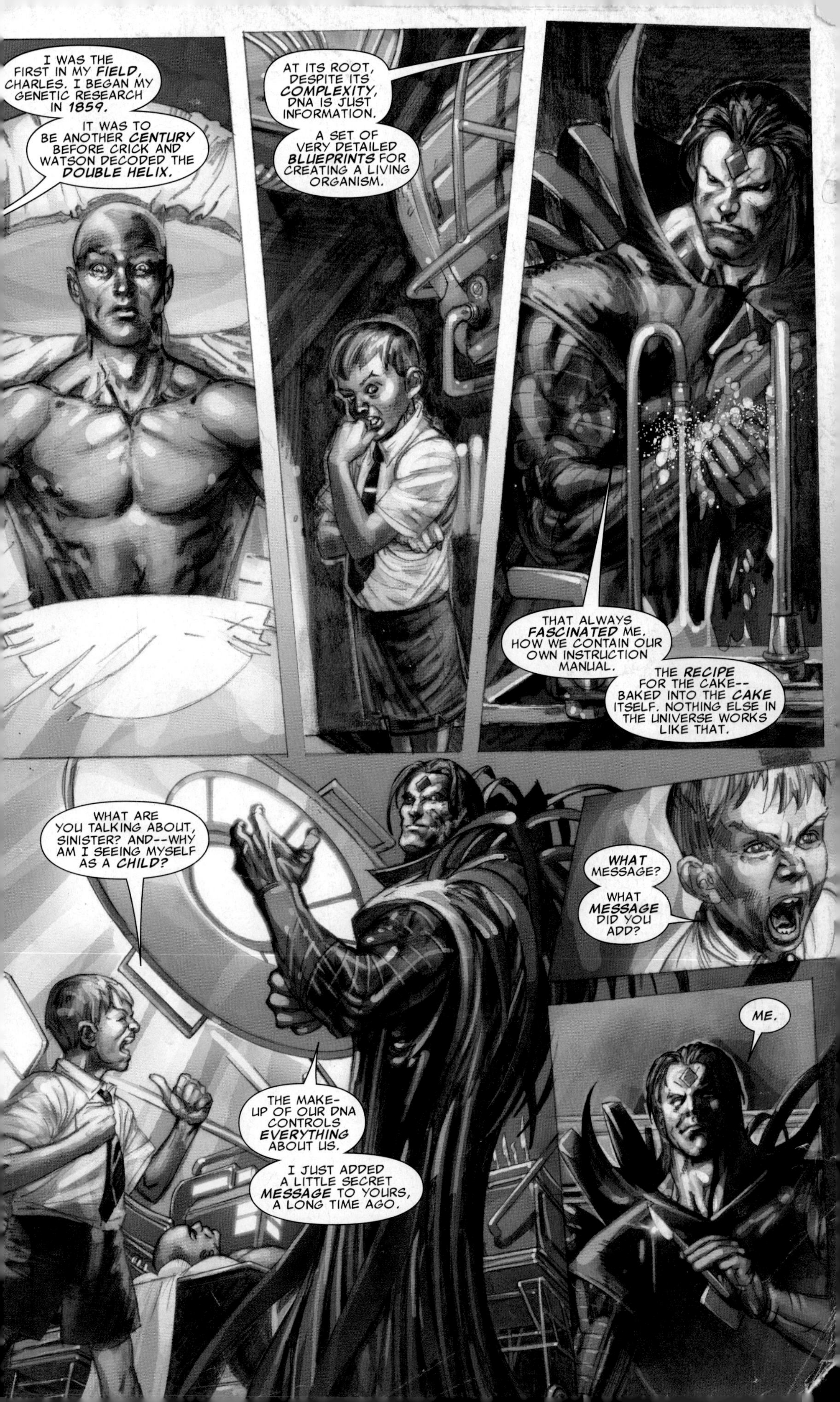

I WAS THE FIRST IN MY FIELD, CHARLES. I BEGAN MY GENETIC RESEARCH IN 1859.
IT WAS TO BE ANOTHER CENTURY BEFORE CRICK AND WATSON DECODED THE DOUBLE HELIX.
AT ITS ROOT, DESPITE ITS COMPLEXITY, DNA IS JUST INFORMATION.
A SET OF VERY DETAILED BLUEPRINTS FOR CREATING A LIVING ORGANISM.
THAT ALWAYS FASCINATED ME. HOW WE CONTAIN OUR OWN INSTRUCTION MANUAL.
THE RECIPE FOR THE CAKE-- BAKED INTO THE CAKE ITSELF. NOTHING ELSE IN THE UNIVERSE WORKS LIKE THAT.
WHAT ARE YOU TALKING ABOUT, SINISTER? AND--WHY AM I SEEING MYSELF AS A CHILD?
THE MAKE-UP OF OUR DNA CONTROLS EVERYTHING ABOUT US.
I JUST ADDED A LITTLE SECRET MESSAGE TO YOURS, A LONG TIME AGO.
WHAT MESSAGE? WHAT MESSAGE DID YOU ADD?
ME.

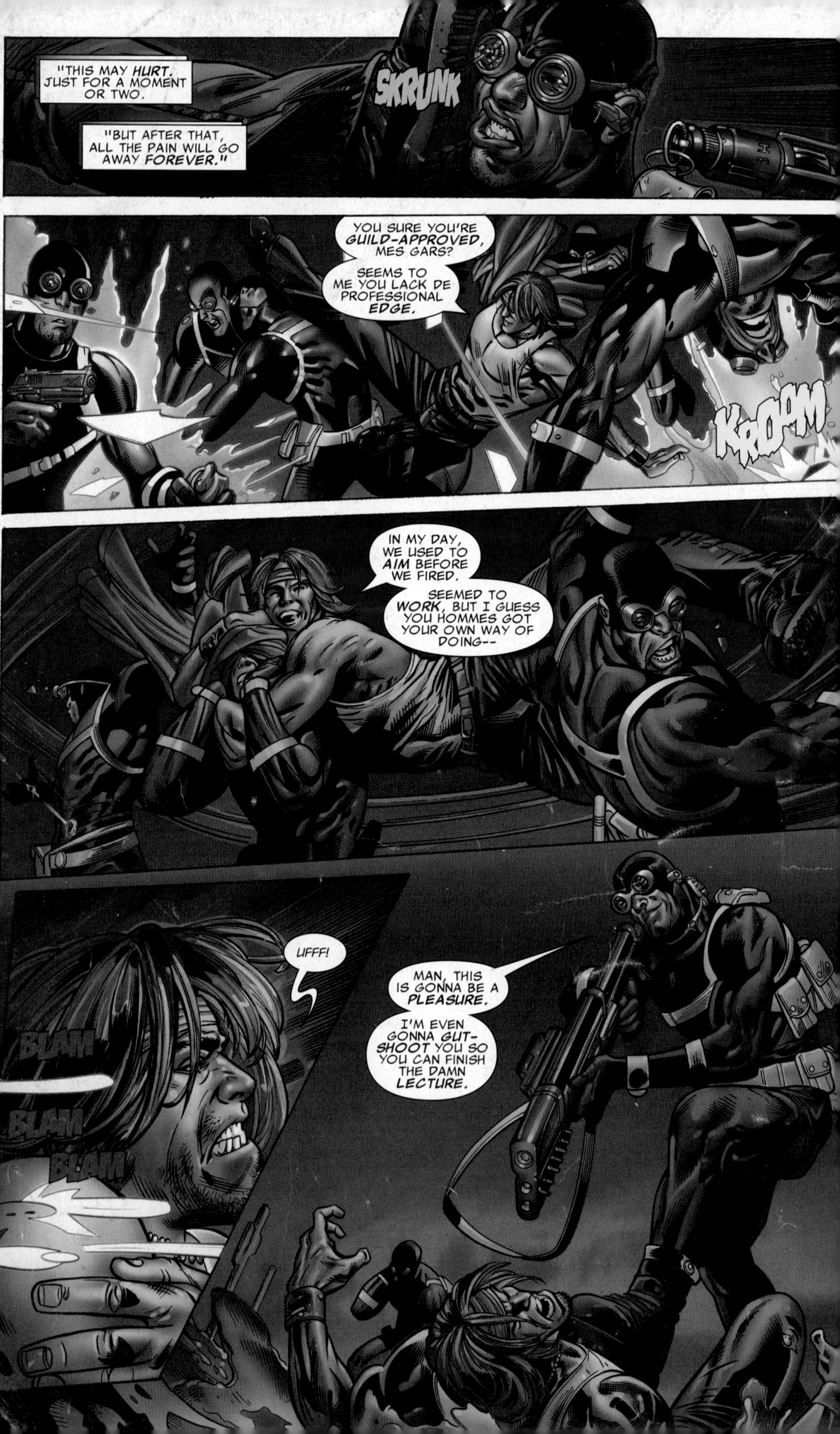
"THIS MAY HURT. JUST FOR A MOMENT OR TWO.
"BUT AFTER THAT, ALL THE PAIN WILL GO AWAY FOREVER."
SKRUNK
YOU SURE YOU'RE GUILD-APPROVED, MES GARS?
SEEMS TO ME YOU LACK DE PROFESSIONAL EDGE.
KROOM
IN MY DAY, WE USED TO AIM BEFORE WE FIRED.
SEEMED TO WORK, BUT I GUESS YOU HOMMES GOT YOUR OWN WAY OF DOING--
UFFF!
BLAM
BLAM
BLAM
MAN, THIS IS GONNA BE A PLEASURE.
I'M EVEN GONNA GUT-SHOOT YOU SO YOU CAN FINISH THE DAMN LECTURE.

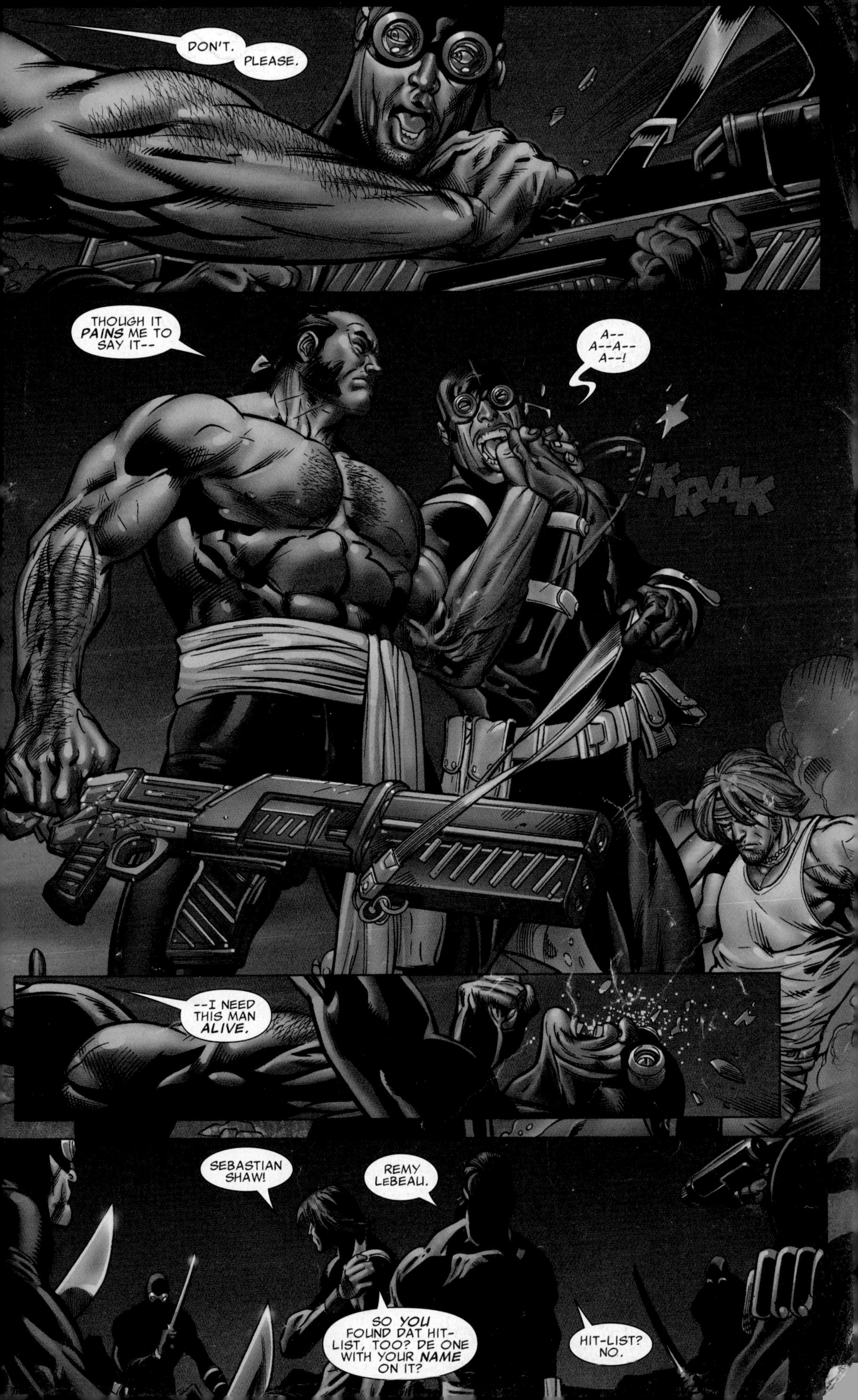
DON'T.
PLEASE.
THOUGH IT PAINS ME TO SAY IT--
A-- A--A-- A--!
KRAK
--I NEED THIS MAN ALIVE.
SEBASTIAN SHAW!
REMY LEBEAU.
SO YOU FOUND DAT HIT-LIST, TOO? DE ONE WITH YOUR NAME ON IT?
HIT-LIST? NO.

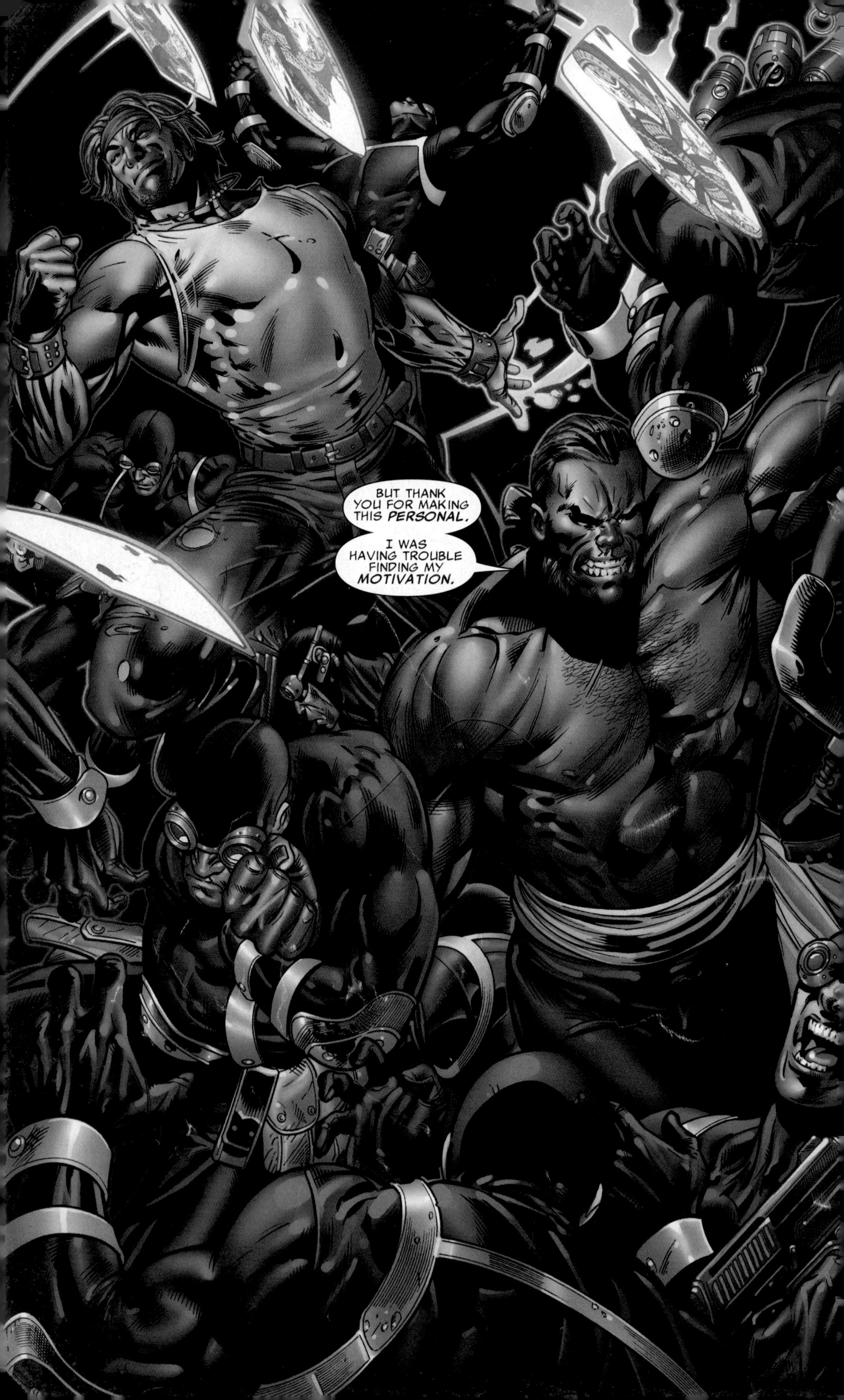
BUT THANK YOU FOR MAKING THIS PERSONAL.
I WAS HAVING TROUBLE FINDING MY MOTIVATION.

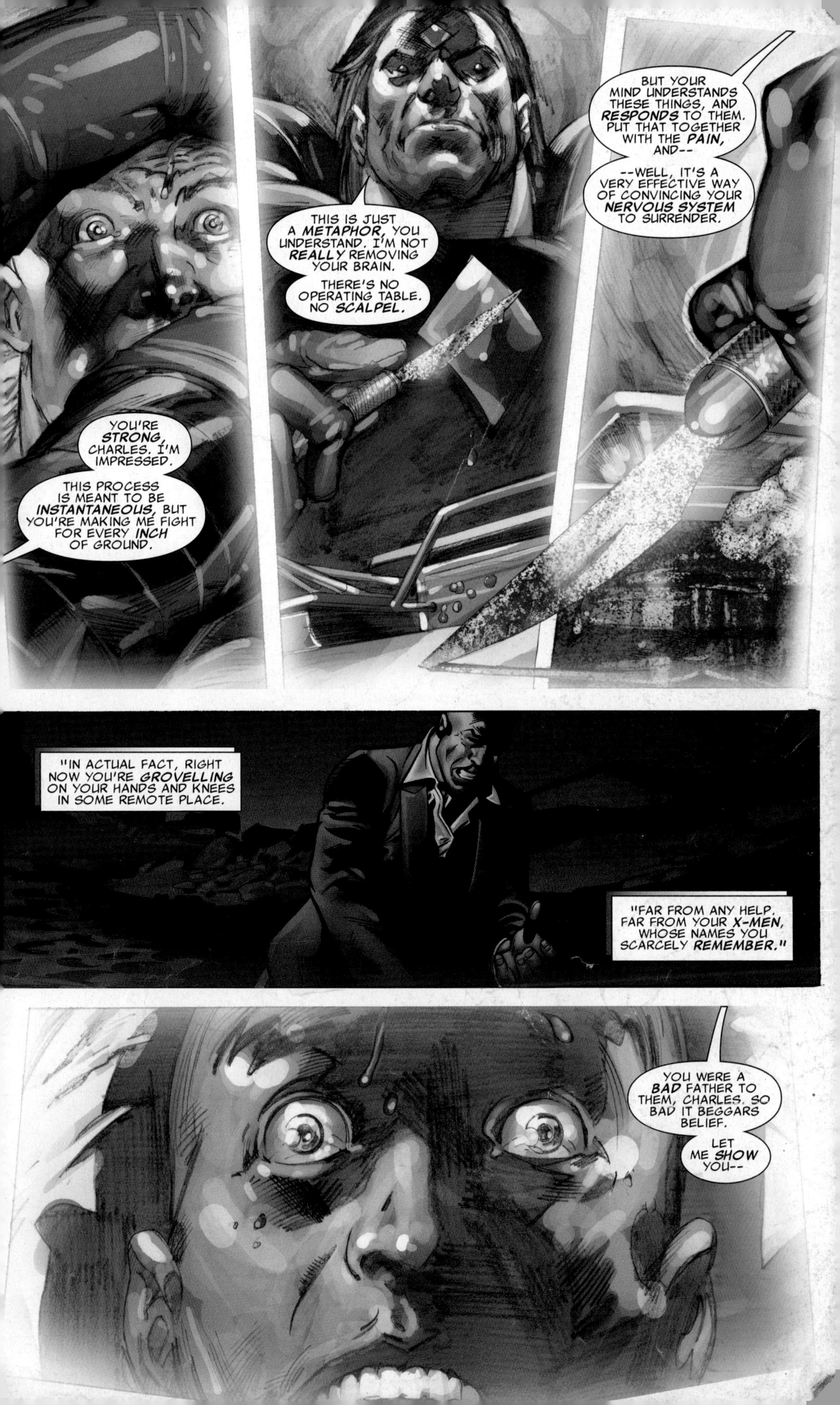
YOU'RE STRONG, CHARLES. I'M IMPRESSED.
THIS PROCESS IS MEANT TO BE INSTANTANEOUS, BUT YOU'RE MAKING ME FIGHT FOR EVERY INCH OF GROUND.
THIS IS JUST A METAPHOR, YOU UNDERSTAND. I'M NOT REALLY REMOVING YOUR BRAIN.
THERE'S NO OPERATING TABLE. NO SCALPEL.
BUT YOUR MIND UNDERSTANDS THESE THINGS, AND RESPONDS TO THEM. PUT THAT TOGETHER WITH THE PAIN, AND--
--WELL, IT'S A VERY EFFECTIVE WAY OF CONVINCING YOUR NERVOUS SYSTEM TO SURRENDER.
"IN ACTUAL FACT, RIGHT NOW YOU'RE GROVELLING ON YOUR HANDS AND KNEES IN SOME REMOTE PLACE.
"FAR FROM ANY HELP. FAR FROM YOUR X-MEN, WHOSE NAMES YOU SCARCELY REMEMBER."
YOU WERE A BAD FATHER TO THEM, CHARLES. SO BAD IT BEGGARS BELIEF.
LET ME SHOW YOU--

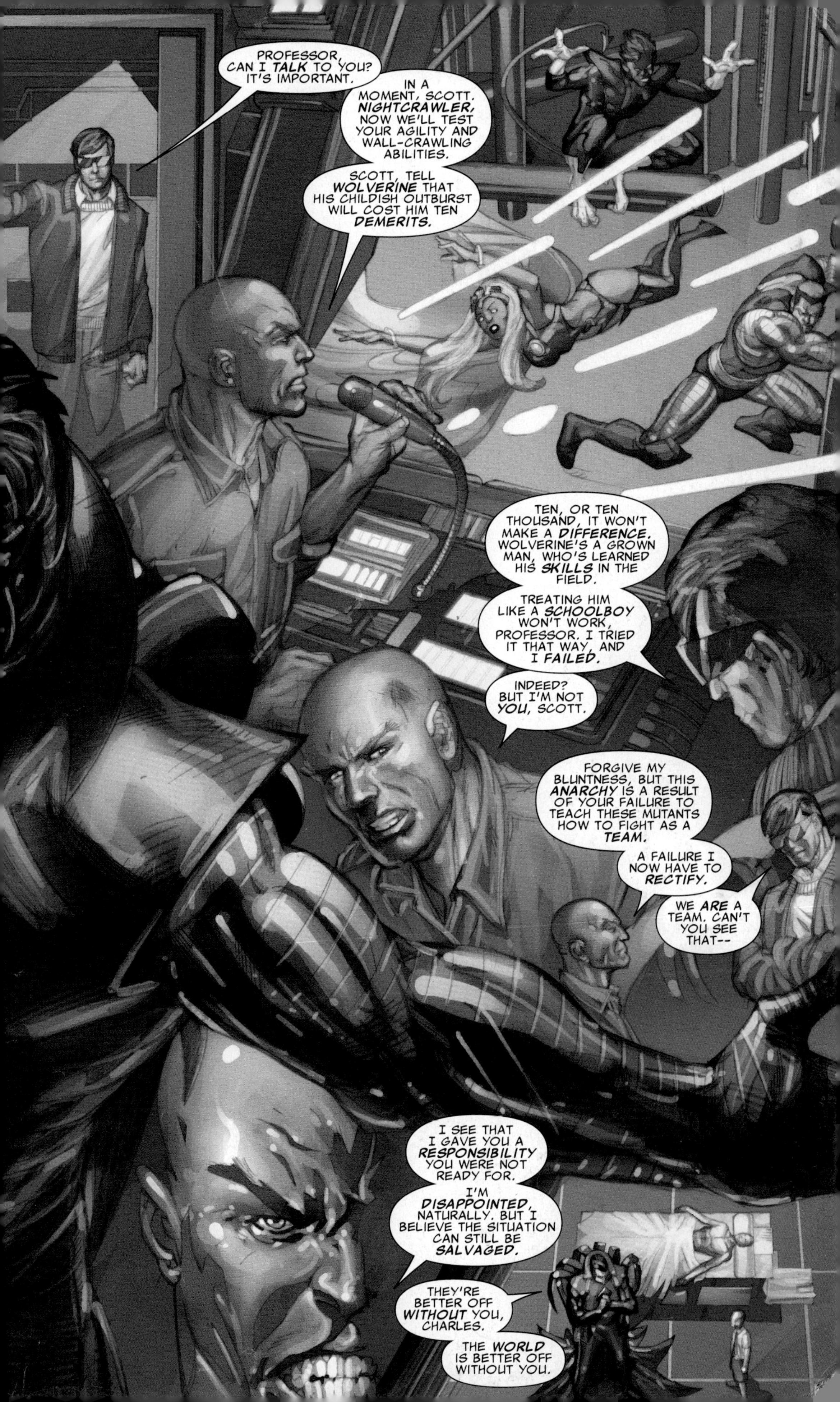
PROFESSOR, CAN I TALK TO YOU? IT'S IMPORTANT.
IN A MOMENT, SCOTT. NIGHTCRAWLER, NOW WE'LL TEST YOUR AGILITY AND WALL-CRAWLING ABILITIES.
SCOTT, TELL WOLVERINE THAT HIS CHILDISH OUTBURST WILL COST HIM TEN DEMERITS.
TEN, OR TEN THOUSAND, IT WON'T MAKE A DIFFERENCE. WOLVERINE'S A GROWN MAN, WHO'S LEARNED HIS SKILLS IN THE FIELD.
TREATING HIM LIKE A SCHOOLBOY WON'T WORK, PROFESSOR. I TRIED IT THAT WAY, AND I FAILED.
INDEED? BUT I'M NOT YOU, SCOTT.
FORGIVE MY BLUNTNESS, BUT THIS ANARCHY IS A RESULT OF YOUR FAILURE TO TEACH THESE MUTANTS HOW TO FIGHT AS A TEAM.
A FAILURE I NOW HAVE TO RECTIFY.
WE ARE A TEAM. CAN'T YOU SEE THAT--
I SEE THAT I GAVE YOU A RESPONSIBILITY YOU WERE NOT READY FOR.
I'M DISAPPOINTED, NATURALLY. BUT I BELIEVE THE SITUATION CAN STILL BE SALVAGED.
THEY'RE BETTER OFF WITHOUT YOU, CHARLES.
THE WORLD IS BETTER OFF WITHOUT YOU.

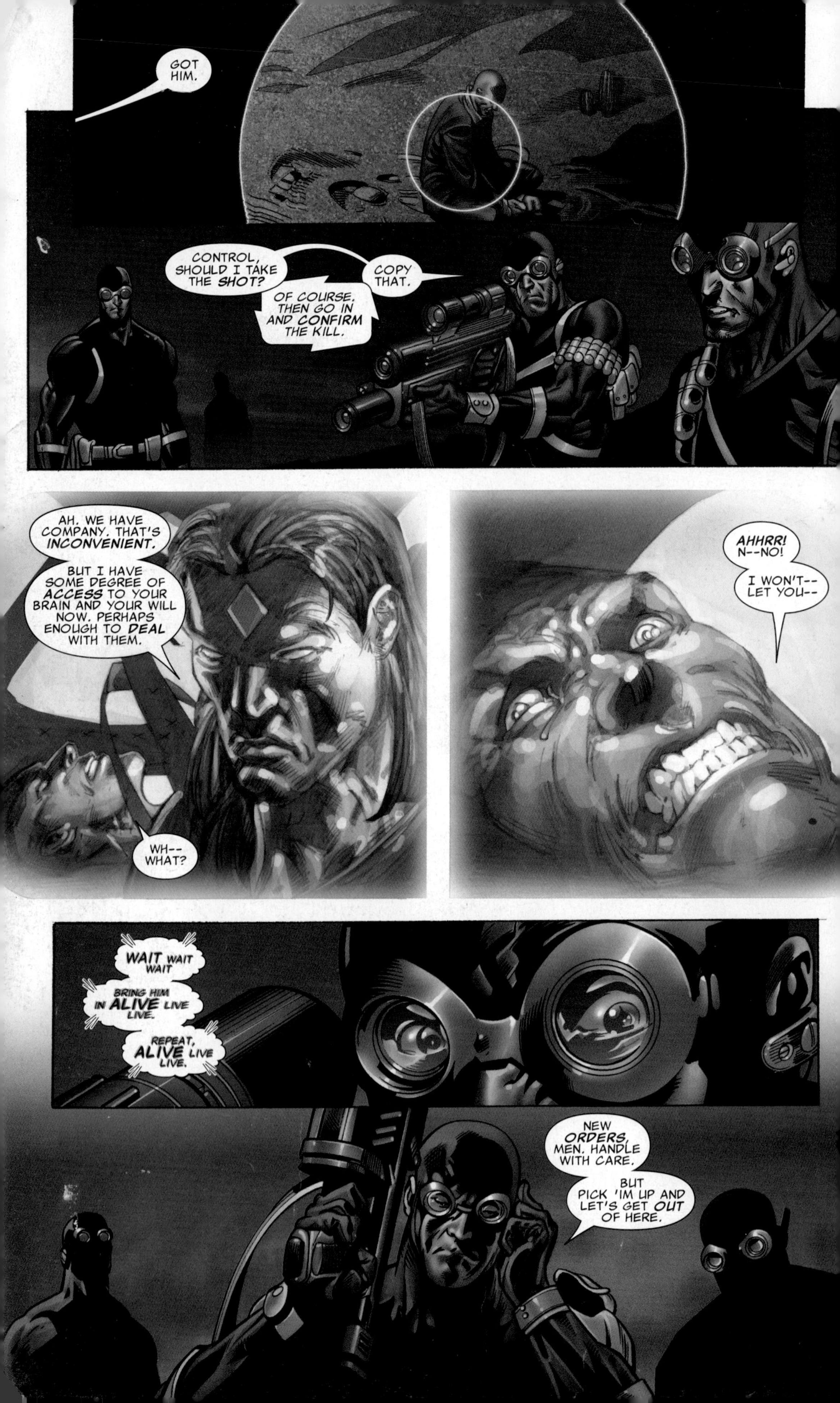
GOT HIM.
CONTROL, SHOULD I TAKE THE SHOT?
OF COURSE. THEN GO IN AND CONFIRM THE KILL.
COPY THAT.
AH. WE HAVE COMPANY. THAT'S INCONVENIENT.
BUT I HAVE SOME DEGREE OF ACCESS TO YOUR BRAIN AND YOUR WILL NOW. PERHAPS ENOUGH TO DEAL WITH THEM.
WH-- WHAT?
AHHRR! N--NO!
I WON'T-- LET YOU--
WAIT WAIT WAIT
BRING HIM IN ALIVE LIVE LIVE.
REPEAT, ALIVE LIVE LIVE.
NEW ORDERS, MEN. HANDLE WITH CARE.
BUT PICK 'IM UP AND LET'S GET OUT OF HERE.

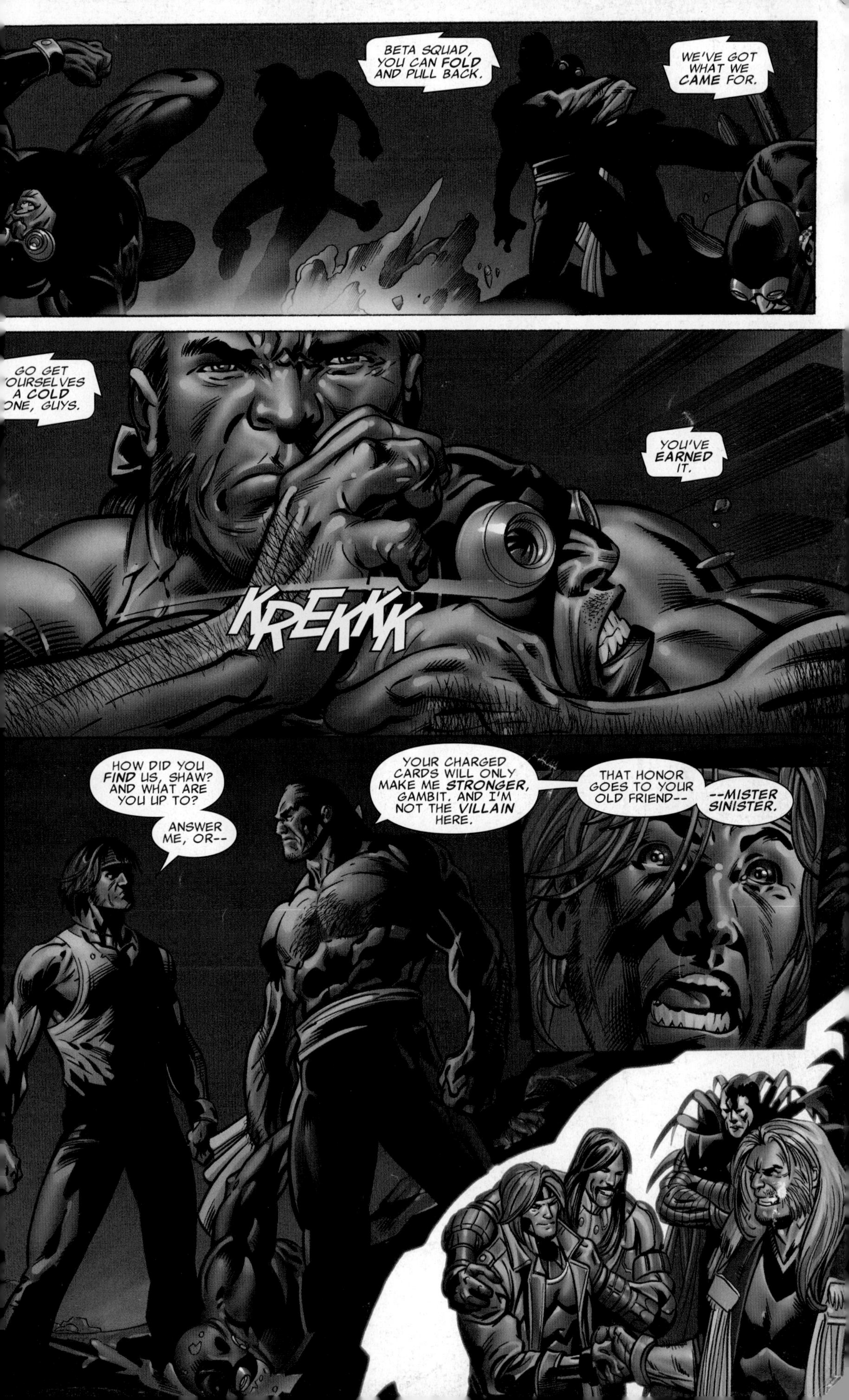
BETA SQUAD, YOU CAN FOLD AND PULL BACK.
WE'VE GOT WHAT WE CAME FOR.
GO GET YOURSELVES A COLD ONE, GUYS.
YOU'VE EARNED IT.
KREKKK
HOW DID YOU FIND US, SHAW? AND WHAT ARE YOU UP TO?
ANSWER ME, OR--
YOUR CHARGED CARDS WILL ONLY MAKE ME STRONGER, GAMBIT. AND I'M NOT THE VILLAIN HERE.
THAT HONOR GOES TO YOUR OLD FRIEND--
--MISTER SINISTER.

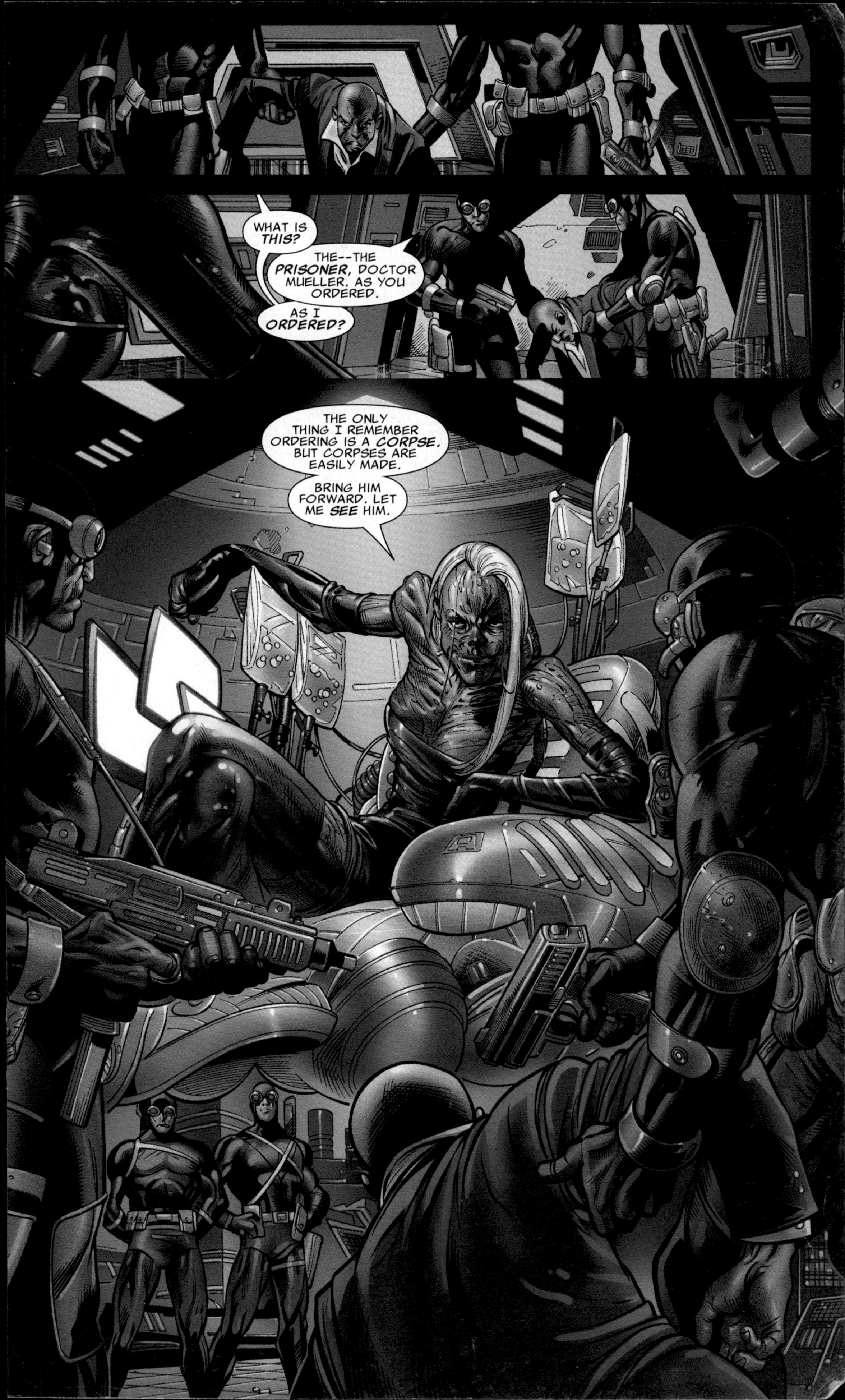
WHAT IS THIS?
THE--THE PRISONER, DOCTOR MUELLER. AS YOU ORDERED.
AS I ORDERED?
THE ONLY THING I REMEMBER ORDERING IS A CORPSE. BUT CORPSES ARE EASILY MADE.
BRING HIM FORWARD. LET ME SEE HIM.

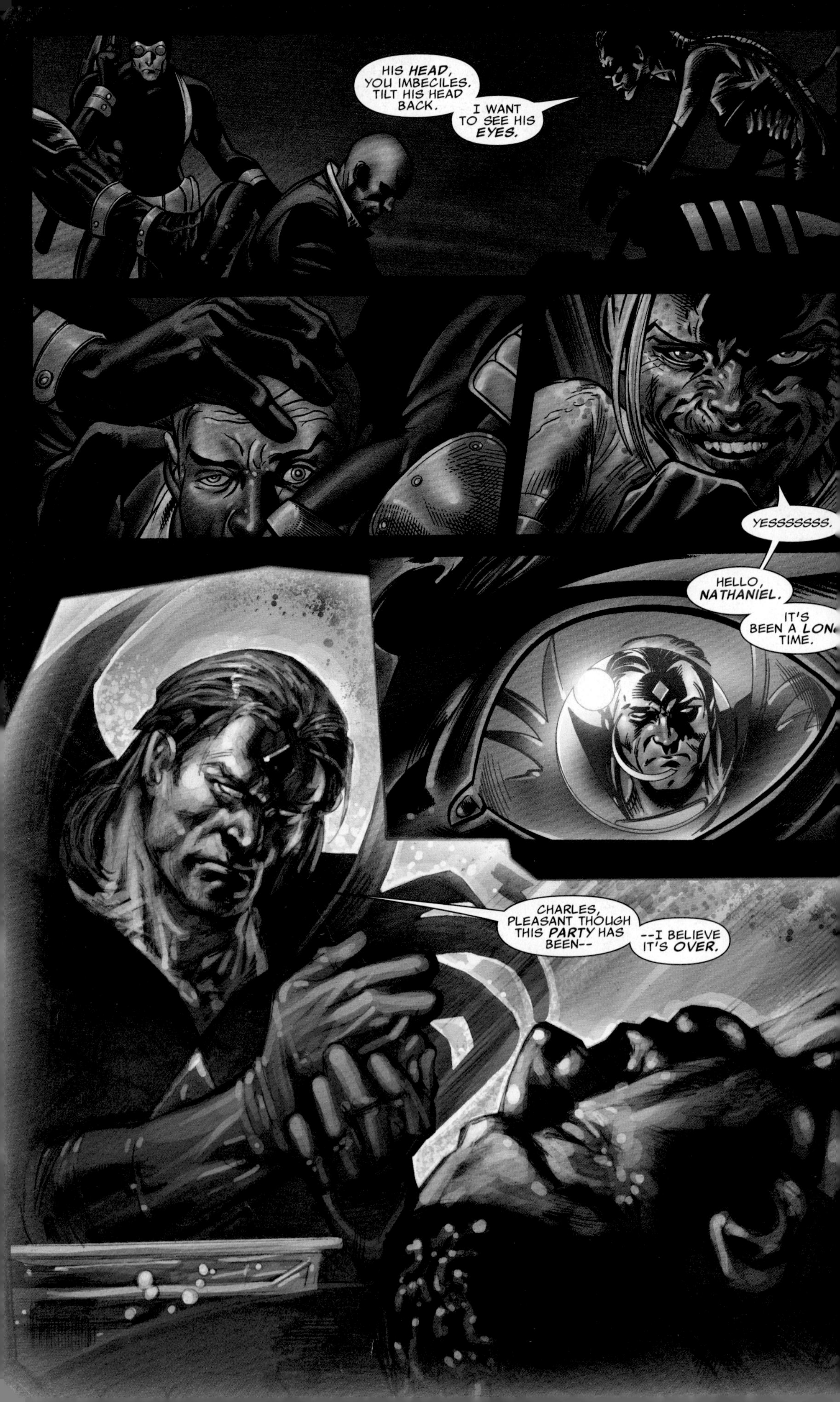
HIS HEAD, YOU IMBECILES. TILT HIS HEAD BACK.
I WANT TO SEE HIS EYES.
YESSSSSSS.
HELLO, NATHANIEL.
IT'S BEEN A LON
TIME.
CHARLES, PLEASANT THOUGH THIS PARTY HAS BEEN--
--I BELIEVE IT'S OVER.

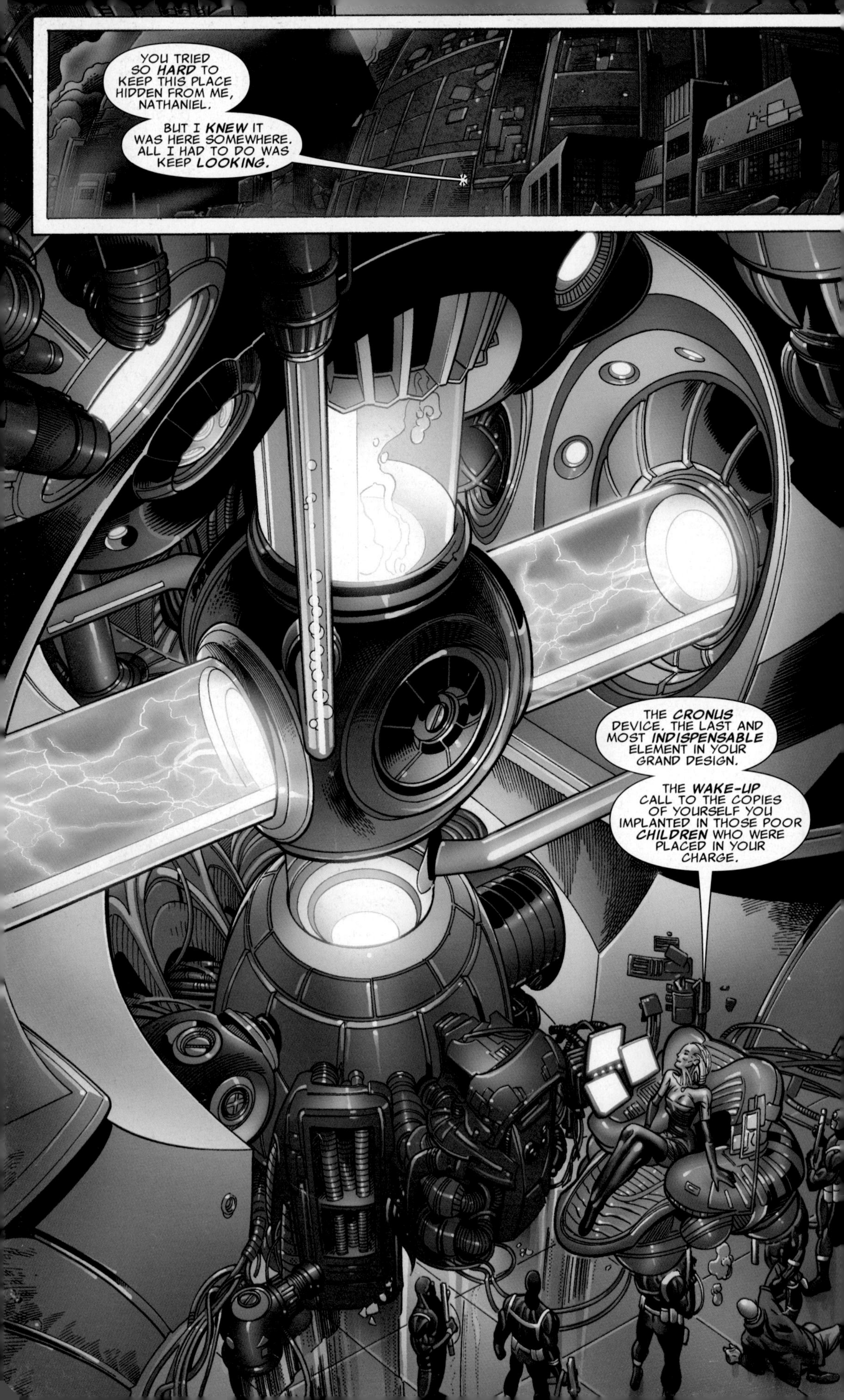
YOU TRIED SO HARD TO KEEP THIS PLACE HIDDEN FROM ME, NATHANIEL.
BUT I KNEW IT WAS HERE SOMEWHERE. ALL I HAD TO DO WAS KEEP LOOKING.
THE CRONUS DEVICE. THE LAST AND MOST INDISPENSABLE ELEMENT IN YOUR GRAND DESIGN.
THE WAKE-UP CALL TO THE COPIES OF YOURSELF YOU IMPLANTED IN THOSE POOR CHILDREN WHO WERE PLACED IN YOUR CHARGE.

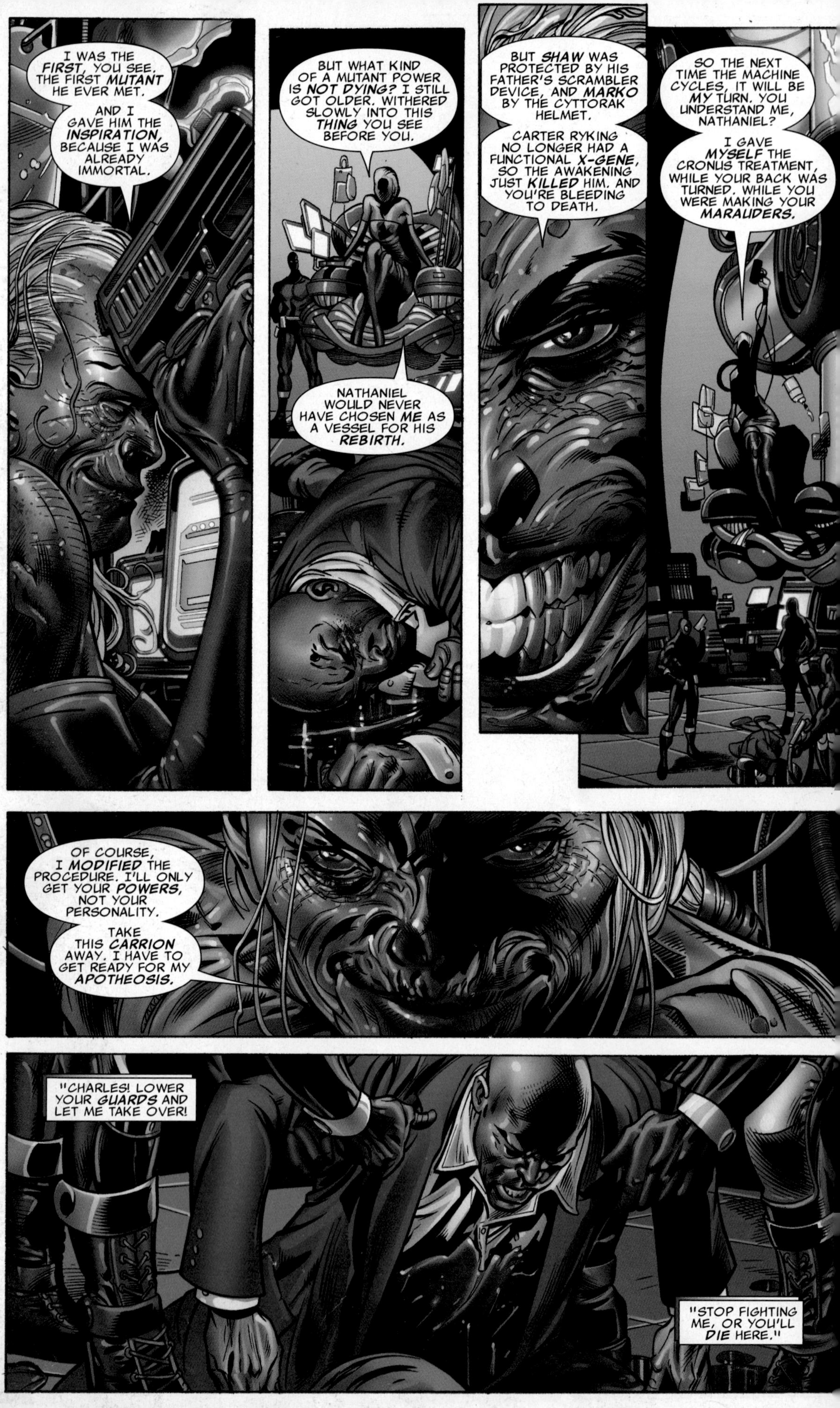
I WAS THE FIRST, YOU SEE. THE FIRST MUTANT HE EVER MET.
AND I GAVE HIM THE INSPIRATION, BECAUSE I WAS ALREADY IMMORTAL.
BUT WHAT KIND OF A MUTANT POWER IS NOT DYING? I STILL GOT OLDER. WITHERED SLOWLY INTO THIS THING YOU SEE BEFORE YOU.
NATHANIEL WOULD NEVER HAVE CHOSEN ME AS A VESSEL FOR HIS REBIRTH.
BUT SHAW WAS PROTECTED BY HIS FATHER'S SCRAMBLER DEVICE, AND MARKO BY THE CYTTORAK HELMET.
CARTER RYKING NO LONGER HAD A FUNCTIONAL X-GENE, SO THE AWAKENING JUST KILLED HIM. AND YOU'RE BLEEDING TO DEATH.
SO THE NEXT TIME THE MACHINE CYCLES, IT WILL BE MY TURN. YOU UNDERSTAND ME, NATHANIEL?
I GAVE MYSELF THE CRONUS TREATMENT, WHILE YOUR BACK WAS TURNED. WHILE YOU WERE MAKING YOUR MARAUDERS.
OF COURSE, I MODIFIED THE PROCEDURE. I'LL ONLY GET YOUR POWERS, NOT YOUR PERSONALITY.
TAKE THIS CARRION AWAY. I HAVE TO GET READY FOR MY APOTHEOSIS.
"CHARLES! LOWER YOUR GUARDS AND LET ME TAKE OVER!
"STOP FIGHTING ME, OR YOU'LL DIE HERE."

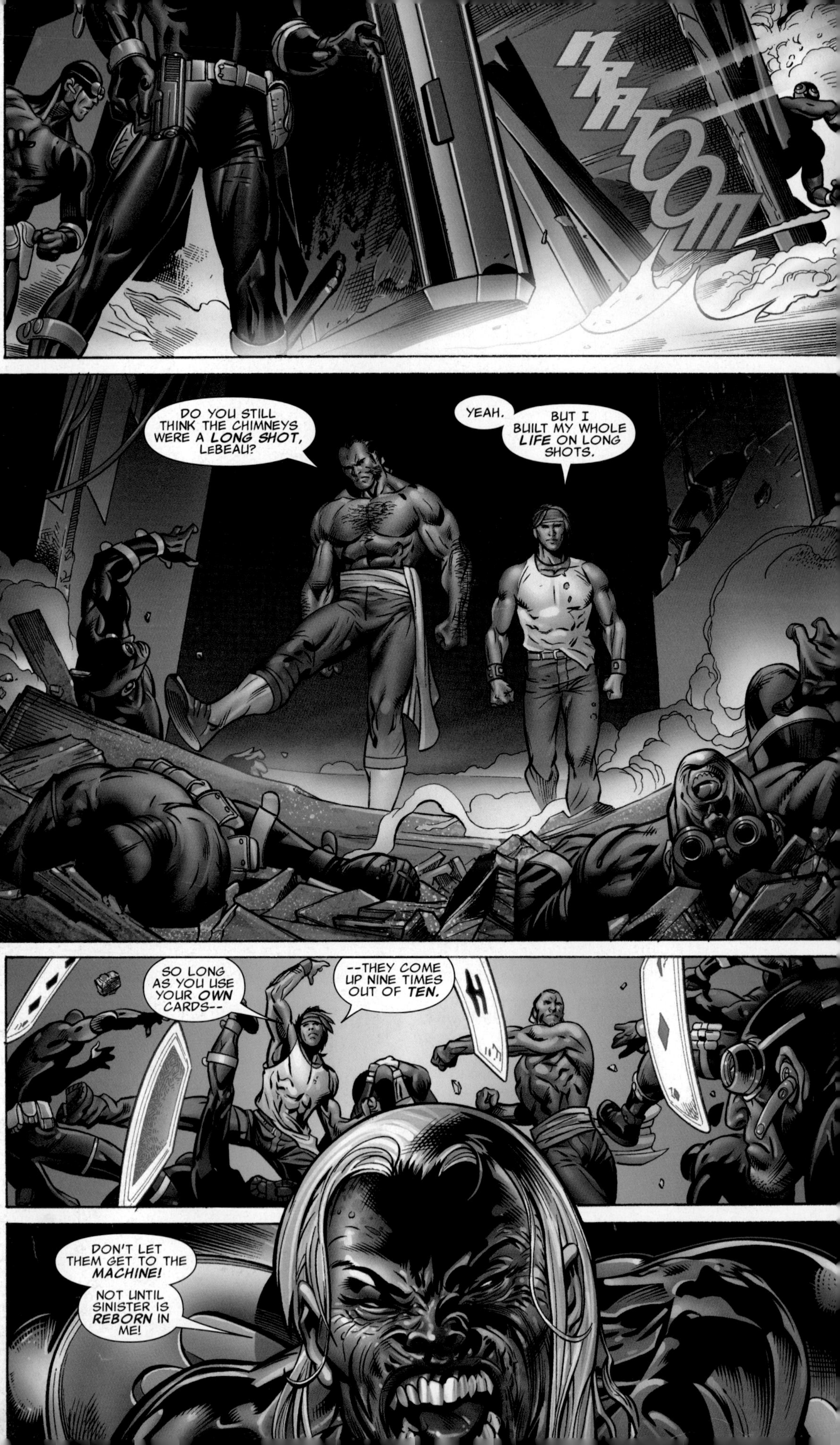
KRAKOOM
DO YOU STILL THINK THE CHIMNEYS WERE A LONG SHOT, LEBEAU?
YEAH.
BUT I BUILT MY WHOLE LIFE ON LONG SHOTS.
SO LONG AS YOU USE YOUR OWN CARDS--
--THEY COME UP NINE TIMES OUT OF TEN.
DON'T LET THEM GET TO THE MACHINE!
NOT UNTIL SINISTER IS REBORN IN ME!

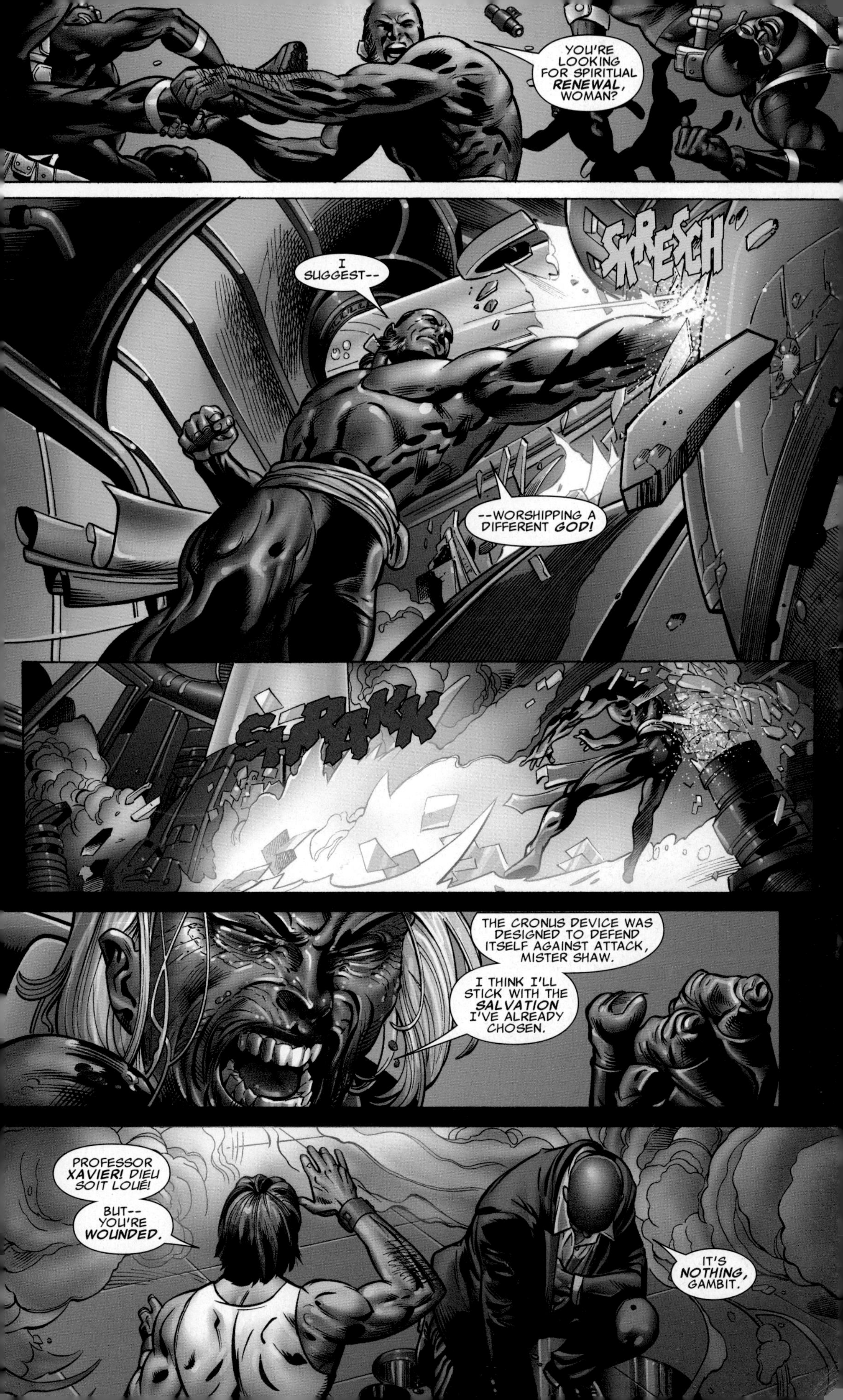

YOU'RE LOOKING FOR SPIRITUAL RENEWAL, WOMAN?
I SUGGEST--
SKRESCH
--WORSHIPPING A DIFFERENT GOD!
SHRAKK
THE CRONUS DEVICE WAS DESIGNED TO DEFEND ITSELF AGAINST ATTACK, MISTER SHAW.
I THINK I'LL STICK WITH THE SALVATION I'VE ALREADY CHOSEN.
PROFESSOR XAVIER! DIEU SOIT LOUÉ!
BUT--YOU'RE WOUNDED.
IT'S NOTHING, GAMBIT.

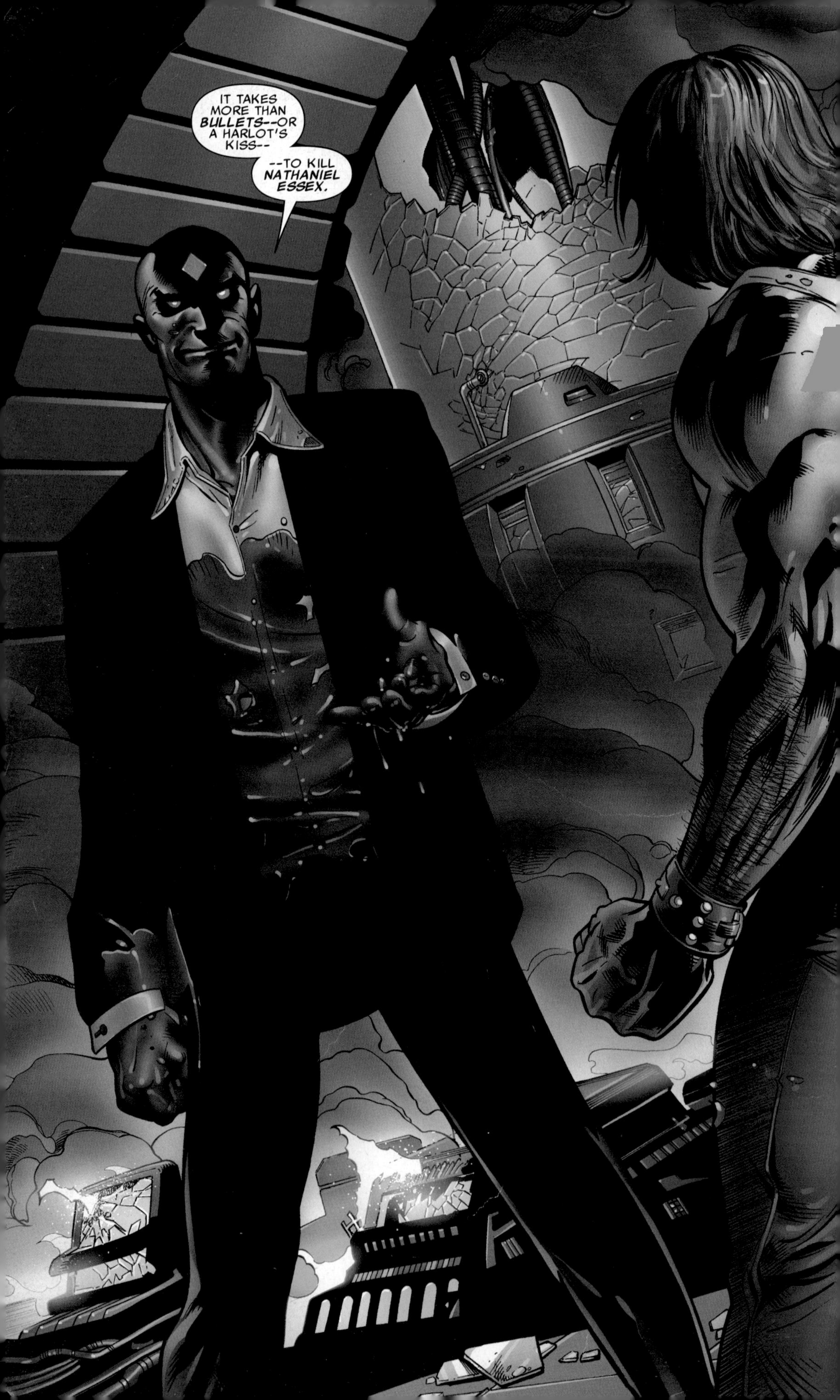
IT TAKES MORE THAN BULLETS--OR A HARLOT'S KISS--
--TO KILL NATHANIEL ESSEX.

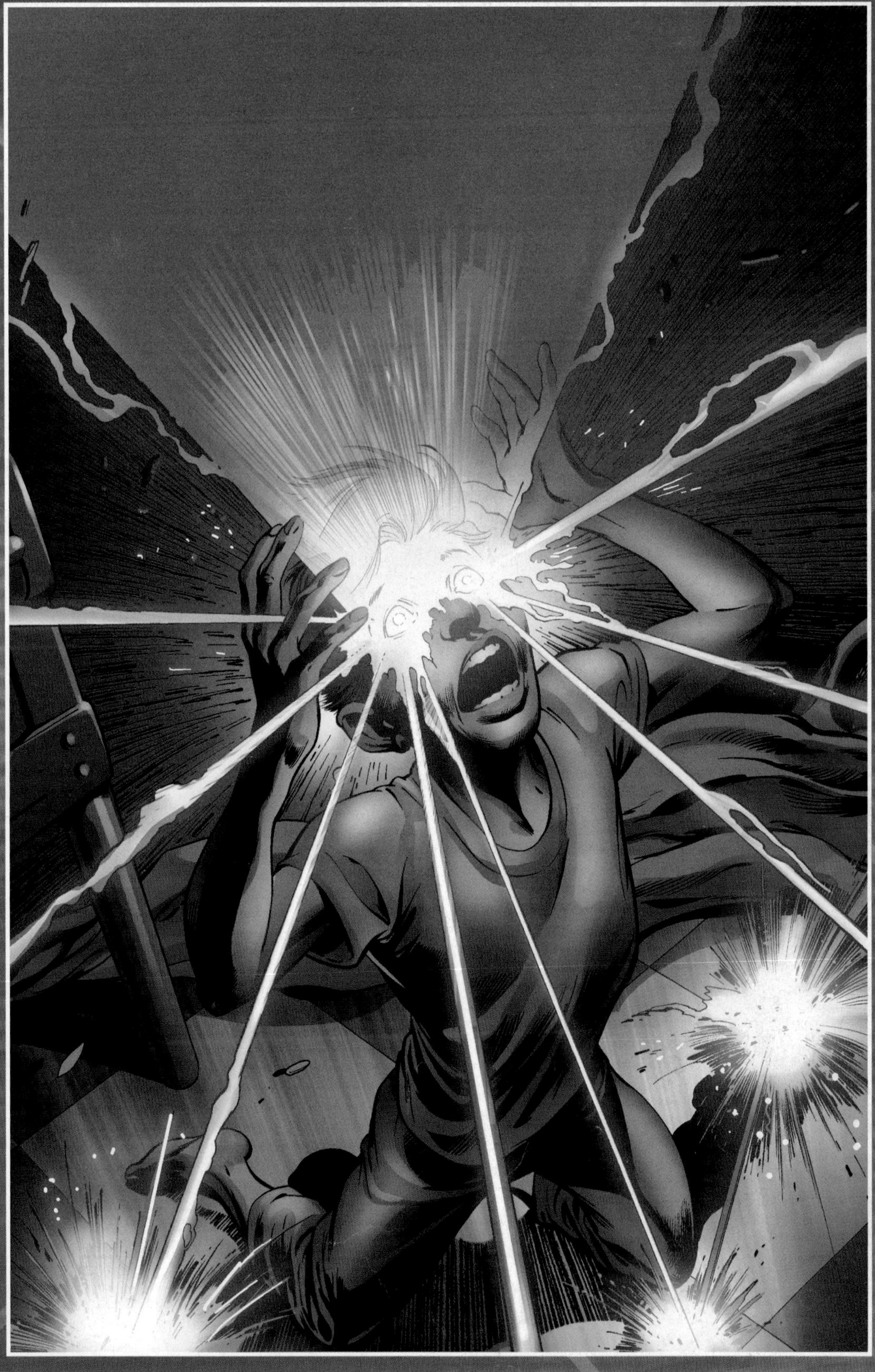

#214

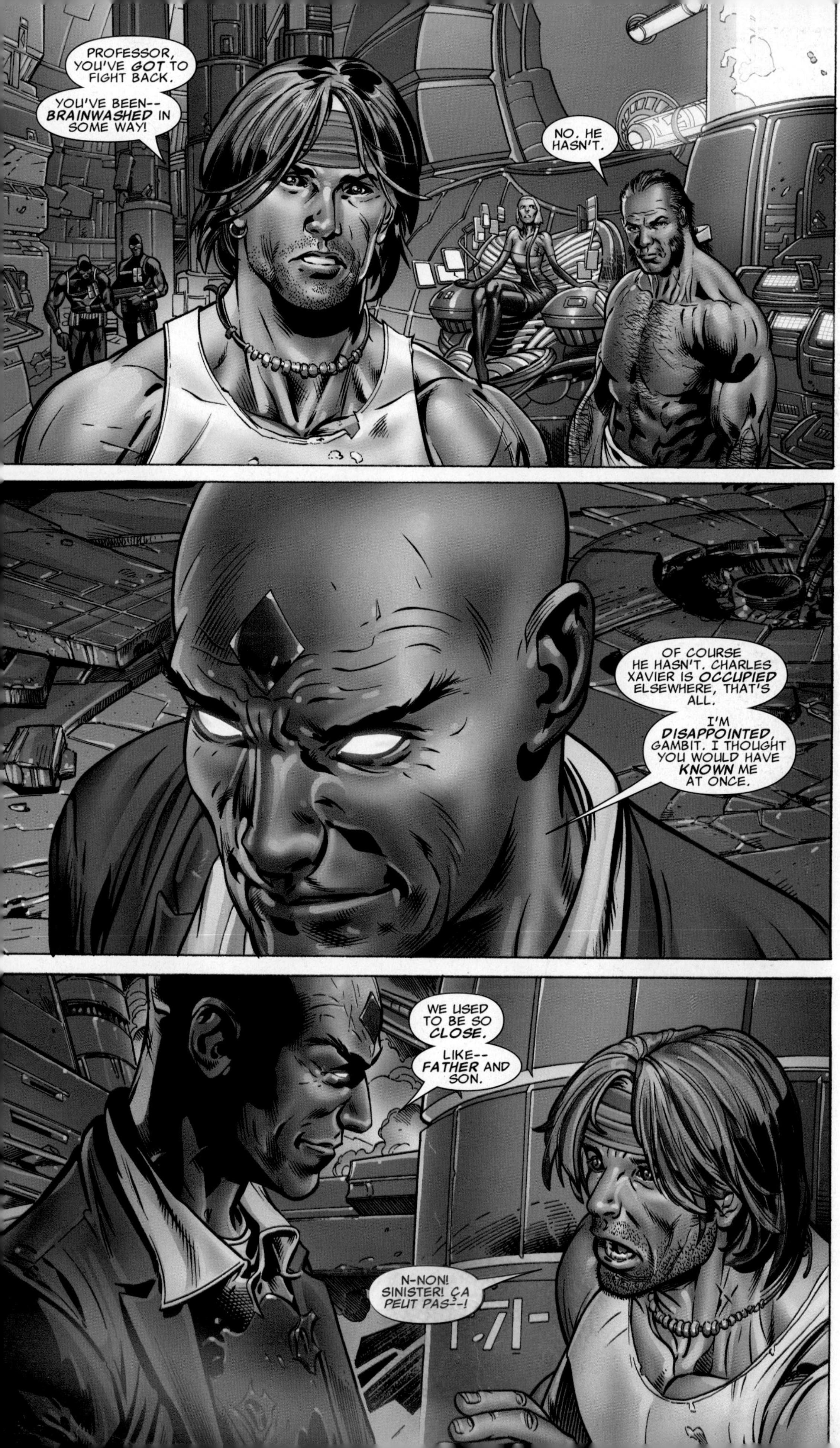
PROFESSOR, YOU'VE GOT TO FIGHT BACK.
YOU'VE BEEN-- BRAINWASHED IN SOME WAY!
NO. HE HASN'T.
OF COURSE HE HASN'T. CHARLES XAVIER IS OCCUPIED ELSEWHERE, THAT'S ALL.
I'M DISAPPOINTED, GAMBIT. I THOUGHT YOU WOULD HAVE KNOWN ME AT ONCE.
WE USED TO BE SO CLOSE.
LIKE-- FATHER AND SON.
N-NON! SINISTER! ÇA PEUT PAS--!

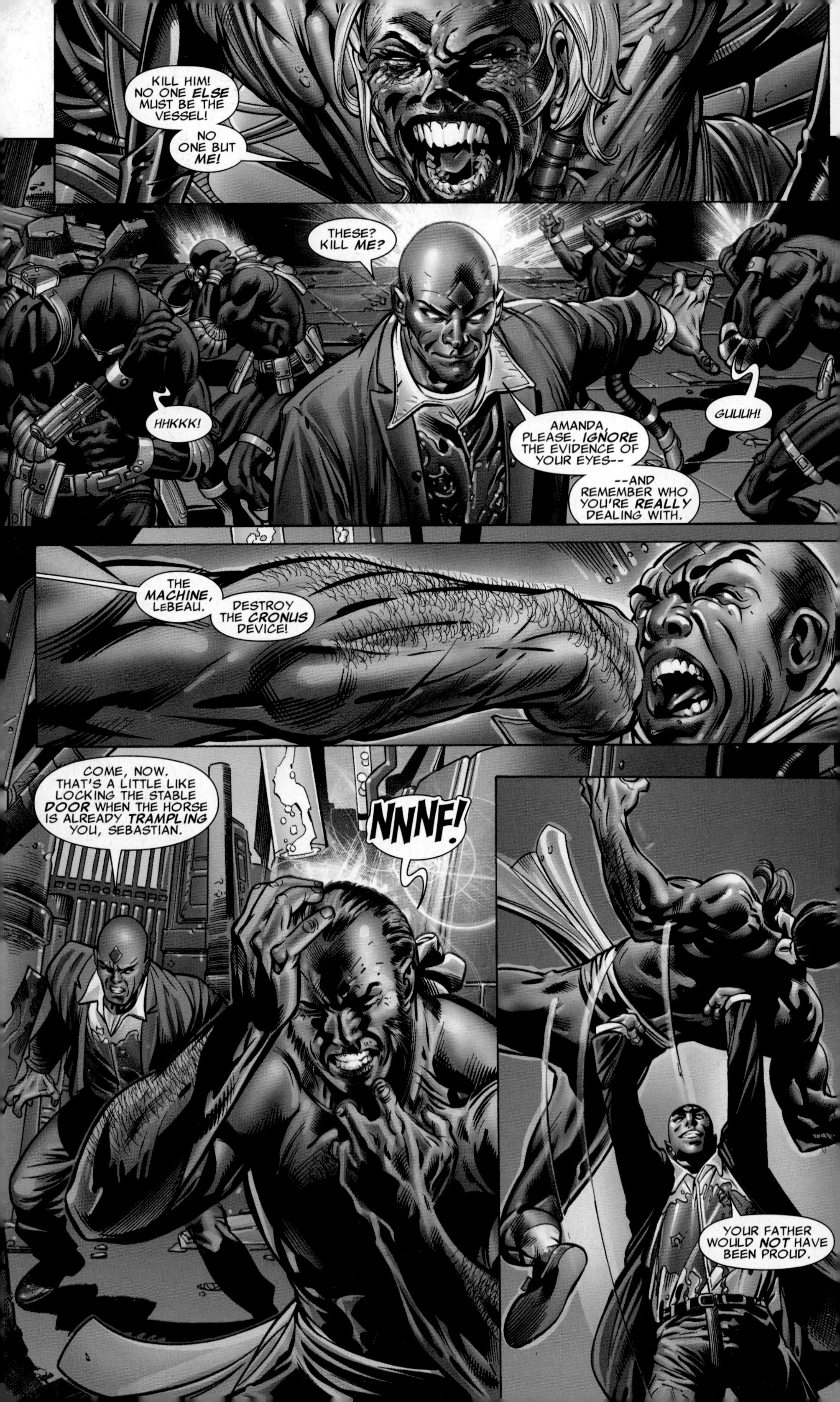
KILL HIM! NO ONE ELSE MUST BE THE VESSEL!
NO ONE BUT ME!
THESE? KILL ME?
HHKKK!
AMANDA, PLEASE. IGNORE THE EVIDENCE OF YOUR EYES--
GUUUH!
--AND REMEMBER WHO YOU'RE REALLY DEALING WITH.
THE MACHINE, LEBEAU.
DESTROY THE CRONUS DEVICE!
COME, NOW. THAT'S A LITTLE LIKE LOCKING THE STABLE DOOR WHEN THE HORSE IS ALREADY TRAMPLING YOU, SEBASTIAN.
NNNF!
YOUR FATHER WOULD NOT HAVE BEEN PROUD.

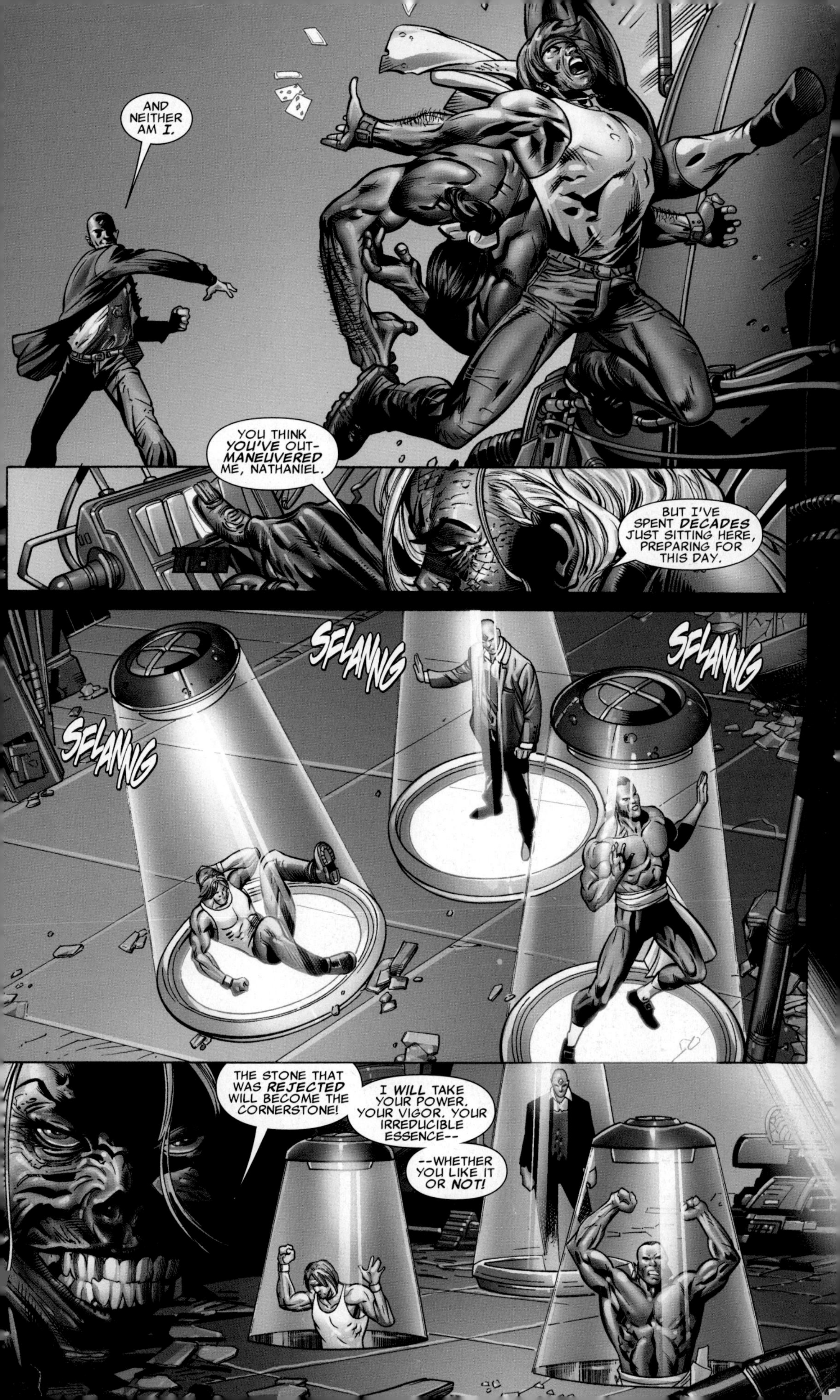
AND NEITHER AM I.
YOU THINK YOU'VE OUT-MANEUVERED ME, NATHANIEL.
BUT I'VE SPENT DECADES JUST SITTING HERE, PREPARING FOR THIS DAY.
SFLANNG
SFLANNG
SFLANNG
THE STONE THAT WAS REJECTED WILL BECOME THE CORNERSTONE!
I WILL TAKE YOUR POWER, YOUR VIGOR, YOUR IRREDUCIBLE ESSENCE--
--WHETHER YOU LIKE IT OR NOT!

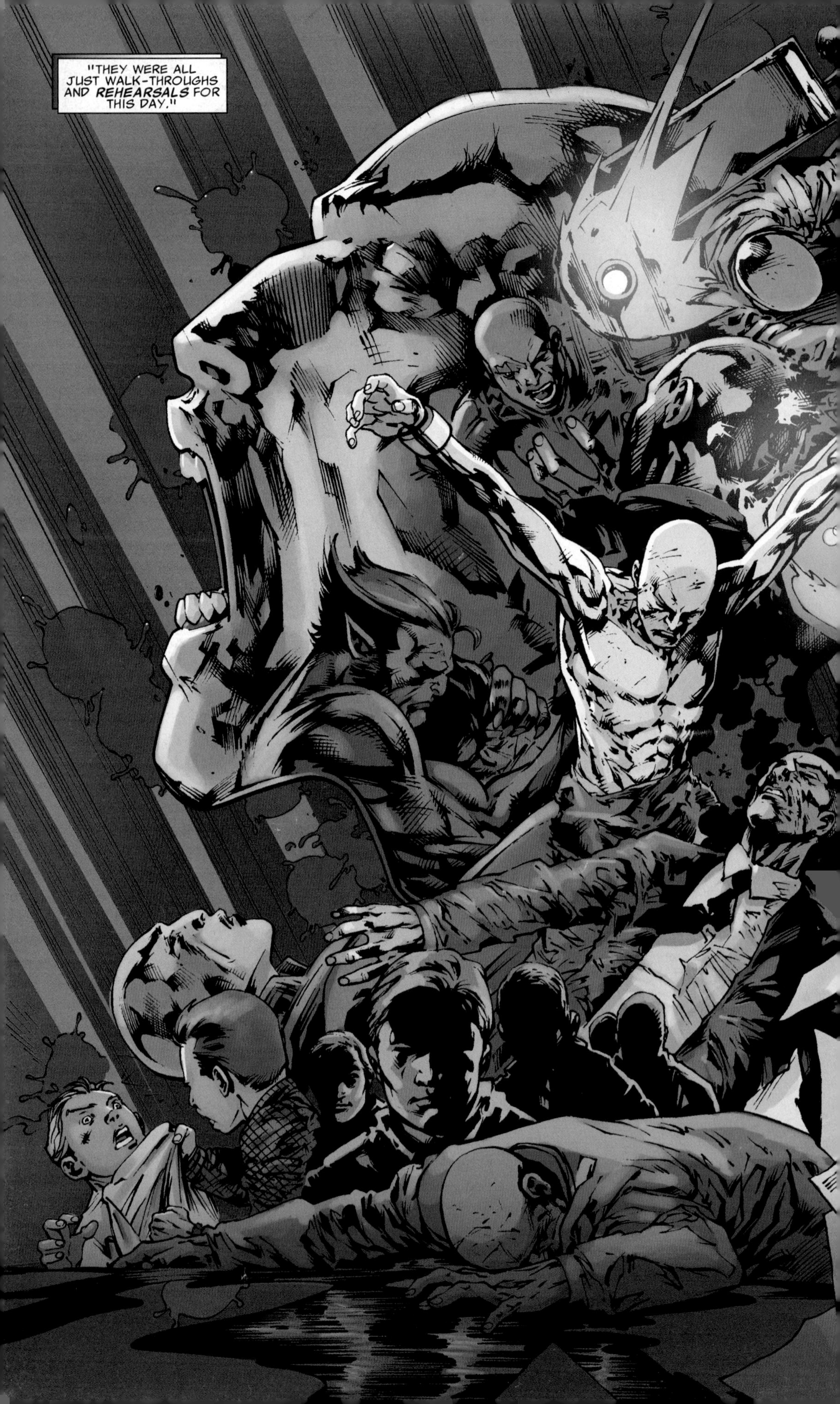
"THEY WERE ALL JUST WALK-THROUGHS AND REHEARSALS FOR THIS DAY."

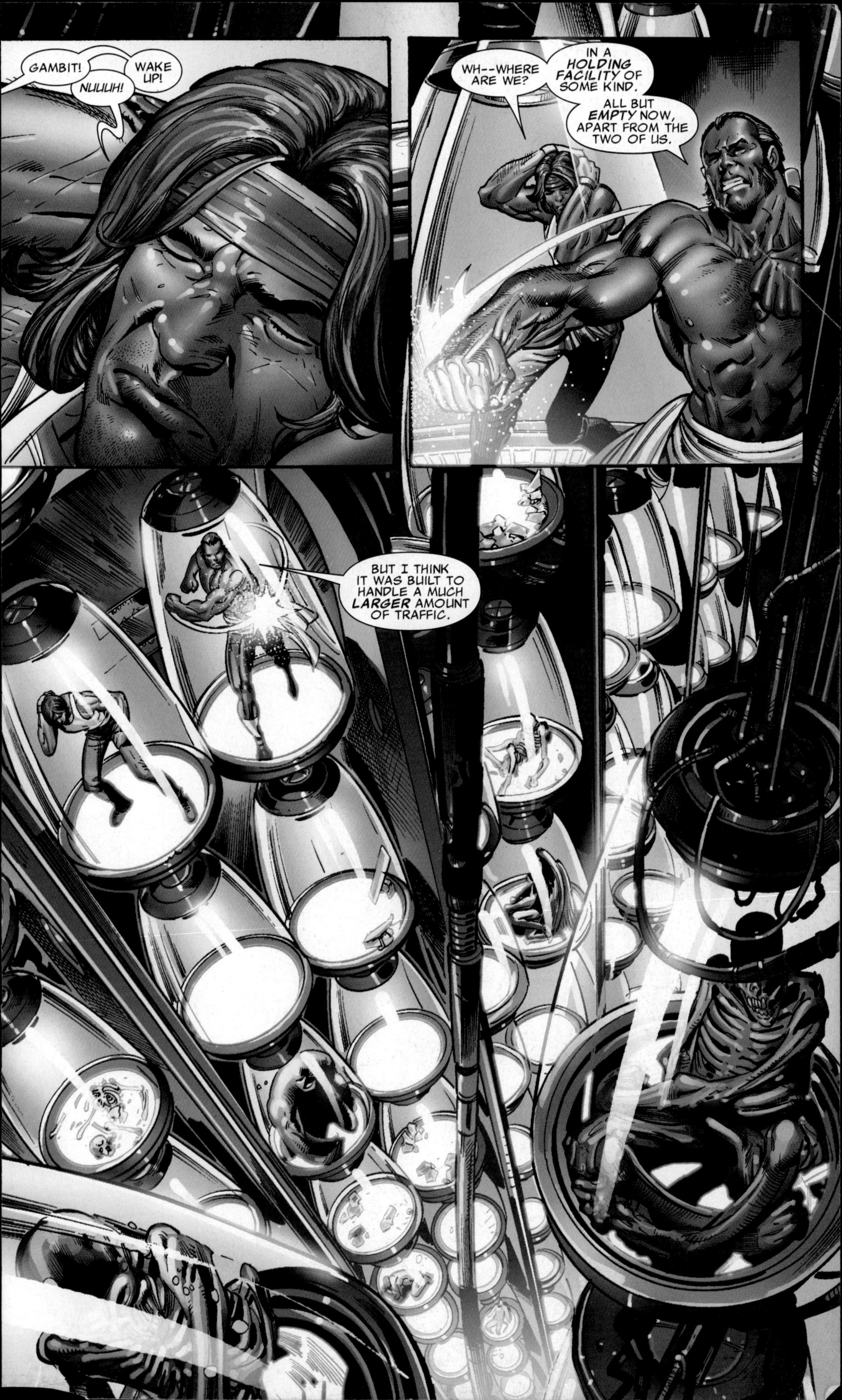
GAMBIT!
NUUUH!
WAKE UP!
WH--WHERE ARE WE?
IN A *HOLDING FACILITY* OF SOME KIND.
ALL BUT *EMPTY* NOW, APART FROM THE TWO OF US.
BUT I THINK IT WAS BUILT TO HANDLE A MUCH *LARGER* AMOUNT OF TRAFFIC.

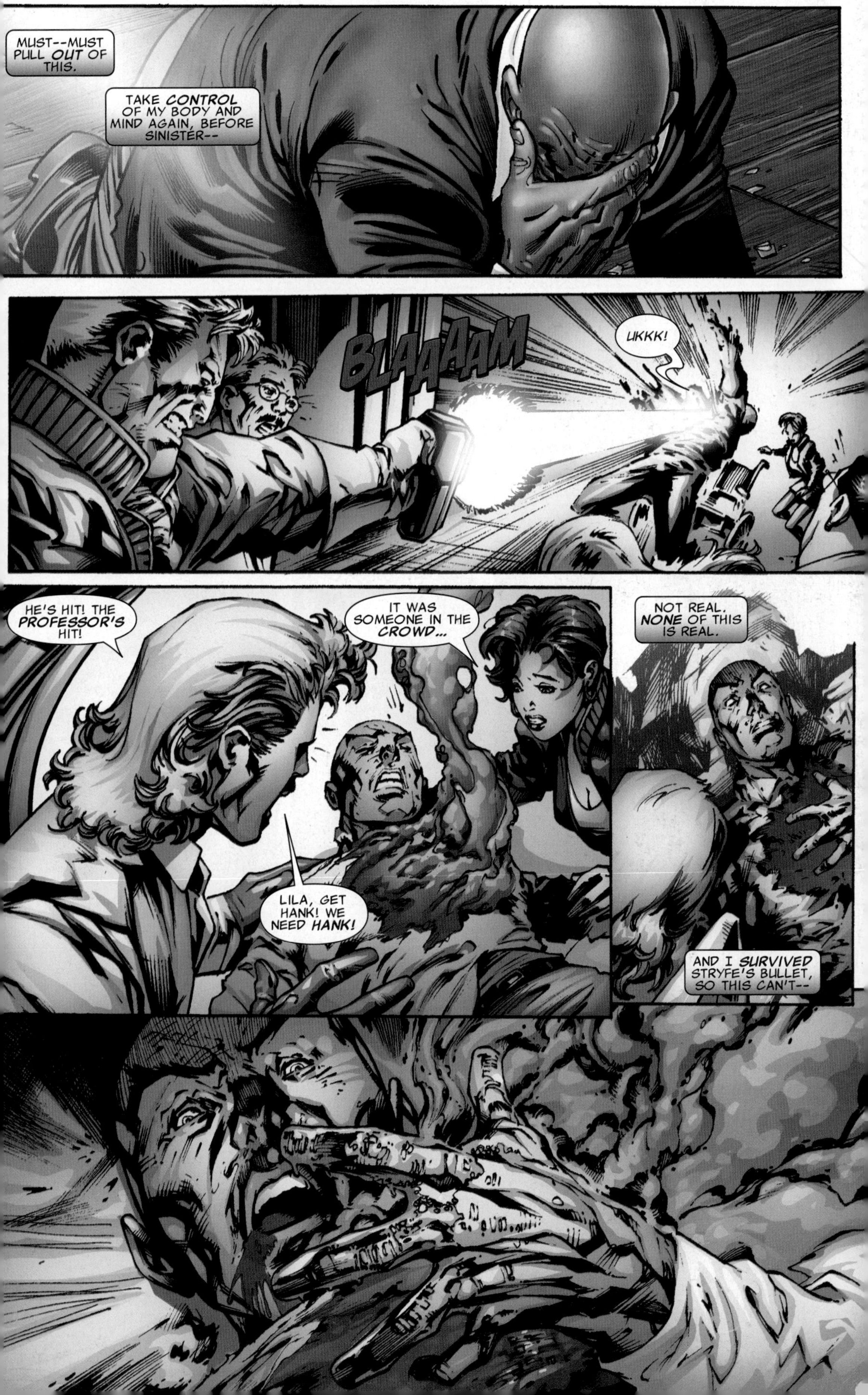

MUST--MUST PULL OUT OF THIS.
TAKE CONTROL OF MY BODY AND MIND AGAIN, BEFORE SINISTER--
BLAAAAM
UKKK!
HE'S HIT! THE PROFESSOR'S HIT!
IT WAS SOMEONE IN THE CROWD...
LILA, GET HANK! WE NEED HANK!
NOT REAL. NONE OF THIS IS REAL.
AND I SURVIVED STRYFE'S BULLET, SO THIS CAN'T--

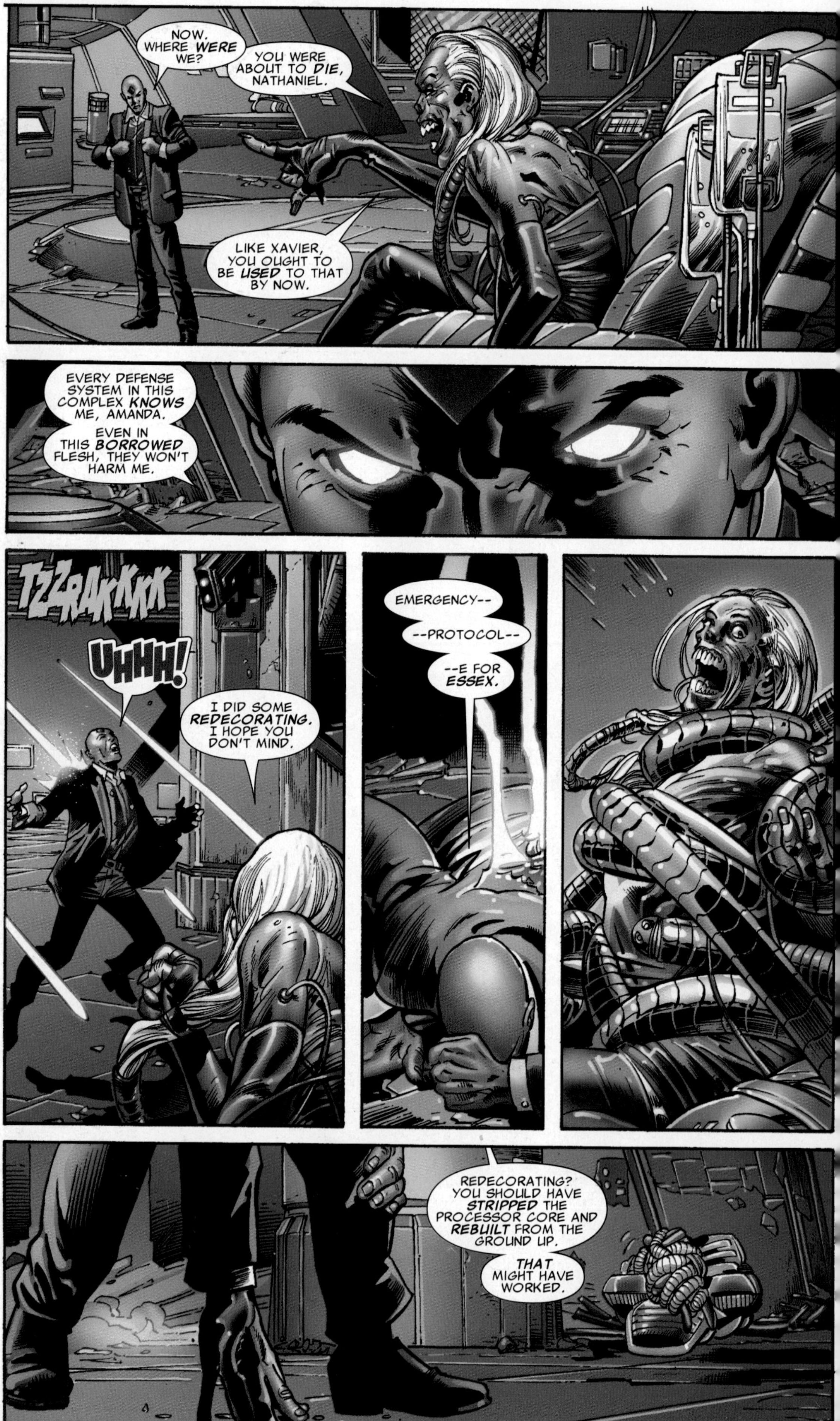
NOW. WHERE WERE WE?
YOU WERE ABOUT TO DIE, NATHANIEL.
LIKE XAVIER, YOU OUGHT TO BE USED TO THAT BY NOW.
EVERY DEFENSE SYSTEM IN THIS COMPLEX KNOWS ME, AMANDA.
EVEN IN THIS BORROWED FLESH, THEY WON'T HARM ME.
TZZRAKKKK
UHHH!
I DID SOME REDECORATING. I HOPE YOU DON'T MIND.
EMERGENCY--
--PROTOCOL--
--E FOR ESSEX.
REDECORATING? YOU SHOULD HAVE STRIPPED THE PROCESSOR CORE AND REBUILT FROM THE GROUND UP.
THAT MIGHT HAVE WORKED.

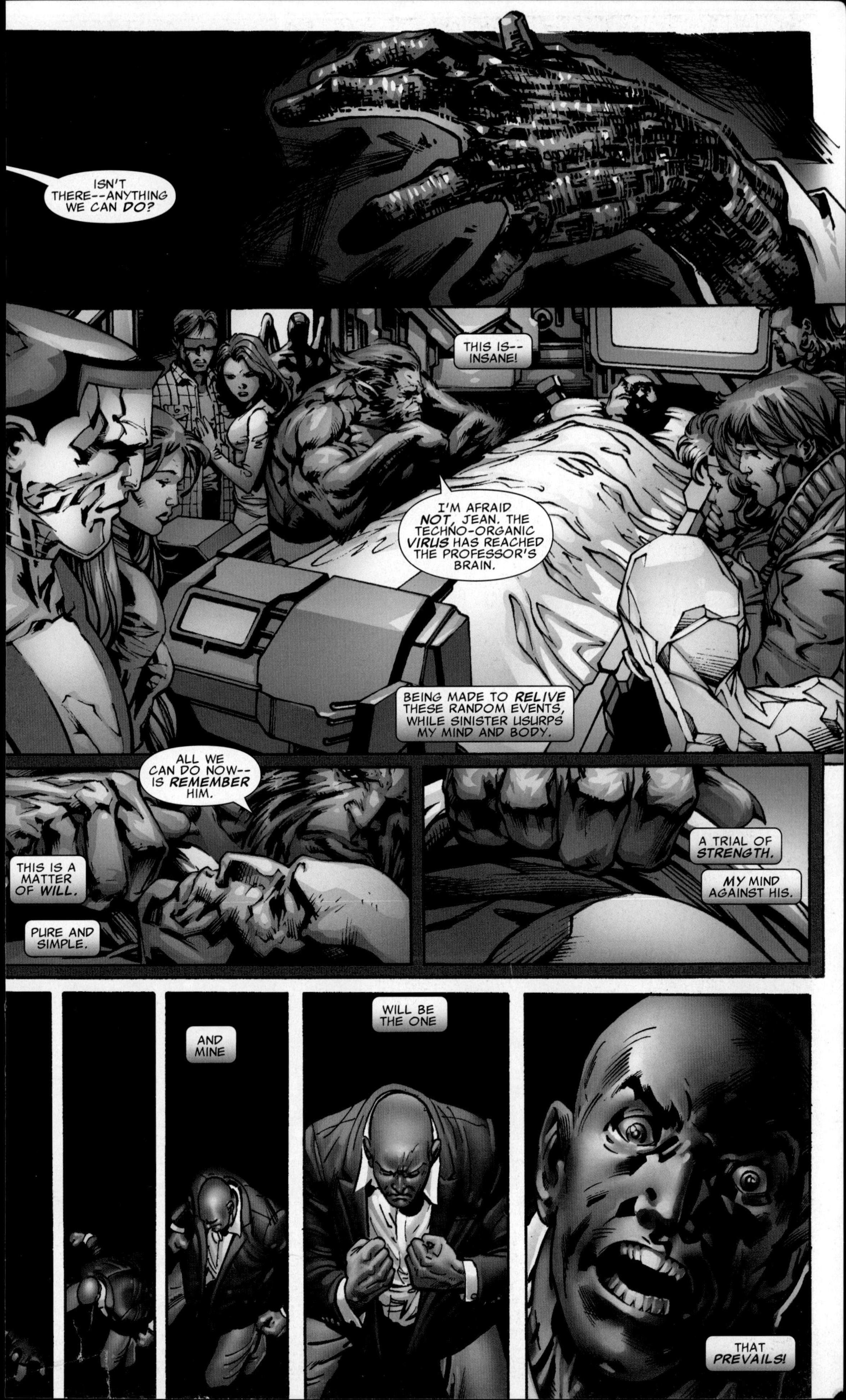
ISN'T THERE--ANYTHING WE CAN DO?
THIS IS-- INSANE!
I'M AFRAID NOT, JEAN. THE TECHNO-ORGANIC VIRUS HAS REACHED THE PROFESSOR'S BRAIN.
BEING MADE TO RELIVE THESE RANDOM EVENTS, WHILE SINISTER USURPS MY MIND AND BODY.
ALL WE CAN DO NOW-- IS REMEMBER HIM.
THIS IS A MATTER OF WILL.
PURE AND SIMPLE.
A TRIAL OF STRENGTH.
MY MIND AGAINST HIS.
AND MINE
WILL BE THE ONE
THAT PREVAILS!

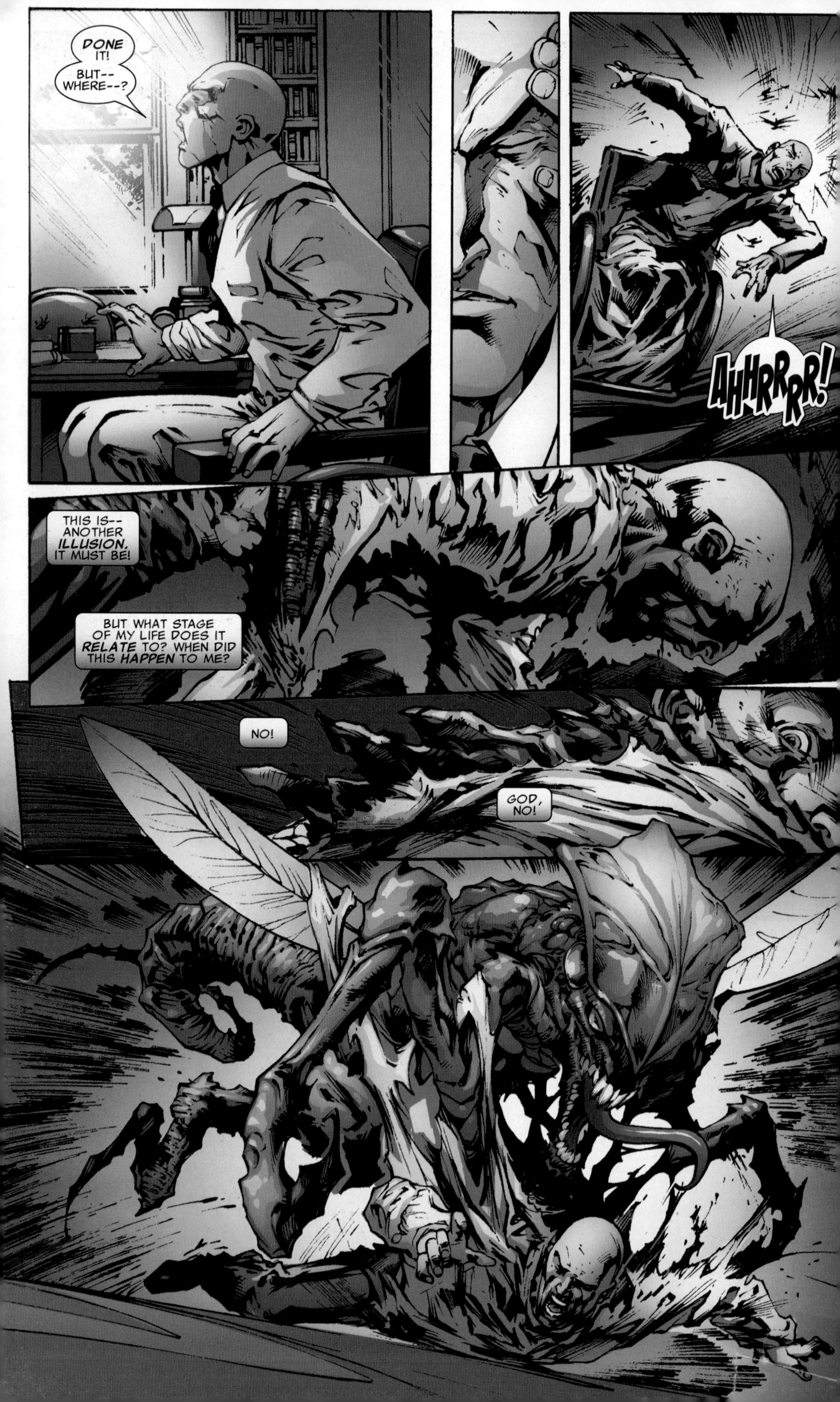
DONE IT! BUT-- WHERE--?
AHHRRRR!
THIS IS-- ANOTHER ILLUSION. IT MUST BE!
BUT WHAT STAGE OF MY LIFE DOES IT RELATE TO? WHEN DID THIS HAPPEN TO ME?
NO!
GOD, NO!

SINISTER! *FACE* ME, YOU COWARD!

FACE YOU, MISTER SHAW? I BELIEVE I ALREADY DID.

AND YOU WERE ONLY *SAVED* BY AMANDA'S INTERVENTION.

SHE'S IN NO *POSITION* TO INTERVENE NOW.

AHHRRR!

SO YOU HAVE MY *UNDIVIDED* ATTENTION.

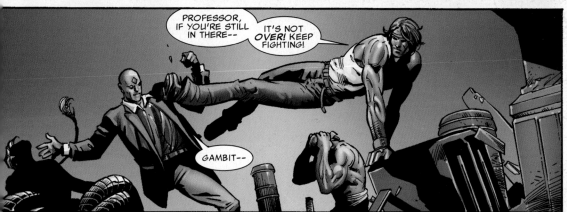

PROFESSOR, IF YOU'RE STILL IN THERE--

IT'S NOT *OVER!* KEEP FIGHTING!

GAMBIT--

I SUGGEST YOU FORGET HOW TO *BREATHE.*

KKHHH!

AND, AS AN *AGREEABLE* SIDE EFFECT-- HOW TO TALK.

THE *BROOD QUEEN* PULLS HERSELF FREE FROM MY BROKEN SHELL, BUT AT THE SAME TIME SHE *IS* ME.

MY MIND AND BODY *DISSOLVED* IN HER LIKE SALT IN WATER. NO LONGER A PRESENCE-- ONLY A FLAVOR.

TELLING ME TO FAIL. SURRENDER. DIE.

THIS--THIS IS WHAT HE'S *DOING.* REMINDING ME OF THE TIMES WHEN MY WILL WAS *SUPPRESSED* AND OVERRIDDEN.

I I I I REFUSE REFUSE REFUSE REFUSE REFUSE *REFUSE!*

ONSLAUGHT? HAH! PERHAPS IF YOU'D *STARTED* WITH ONSLAUGHT.

BUT NOW? TOO *OBVIOUS* A MOVE, SINISTER.

AND THE CHILD YOU *TERRORIZED* HAS FINALLY STEPPED OUT OF YOUR *SHADOW.*

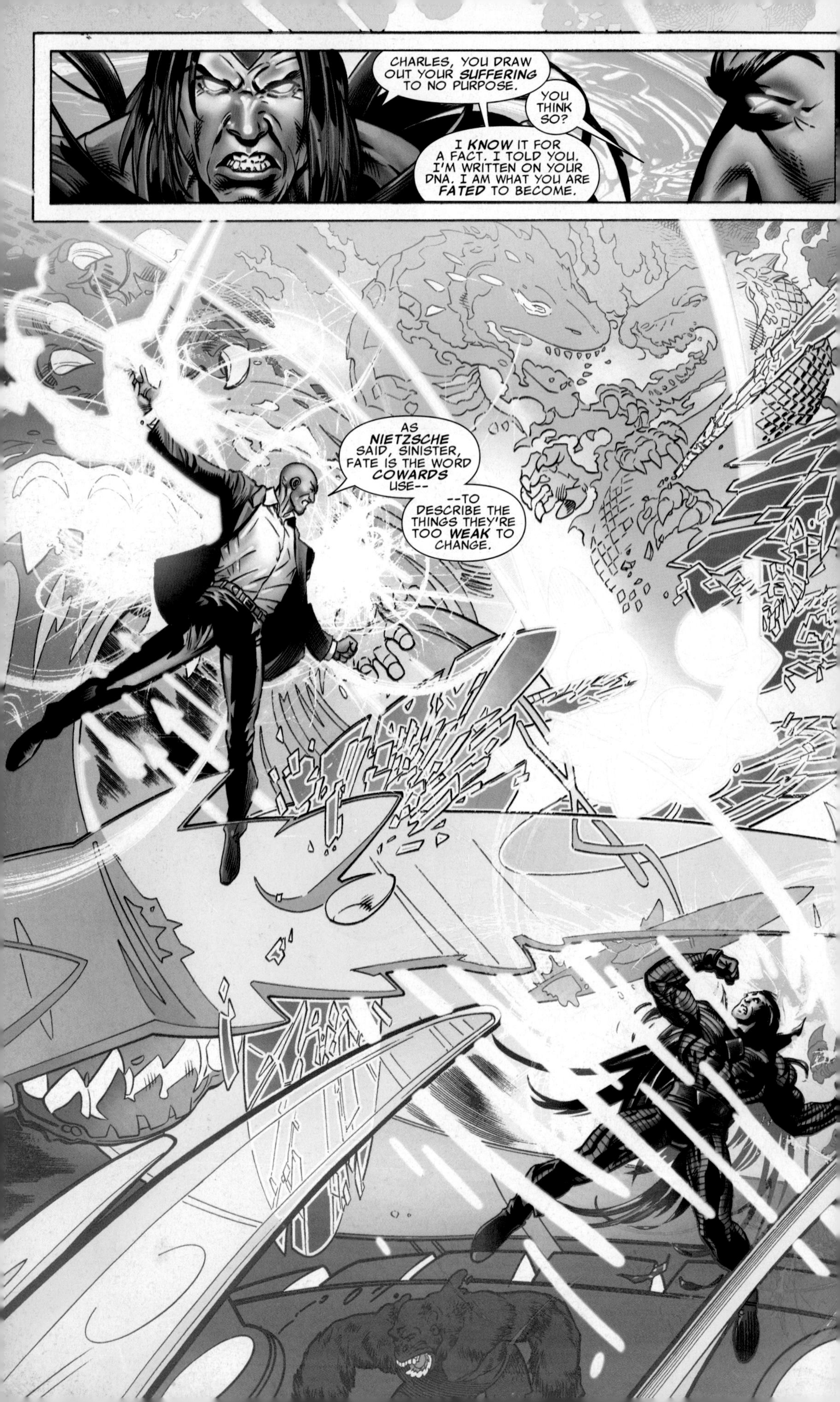

CHARLES, YOU DRAW OUT YOUR SUFFERING TO NO PURPOSE.
YOU THINK SO?
I KNOW IT FOR A FACT. I TOLD YOU. I'M WRITTEN ON YOUR DNA. I AM WHAT YOU ARE FATED TO BECOME.
AS NIETZSCHE SAID, SINISTER, FATE IS THE WORD COWARDS USE--
--TO DESCRIBE THE THINGS THEY'RE TOO WEAK TO CHANGE.

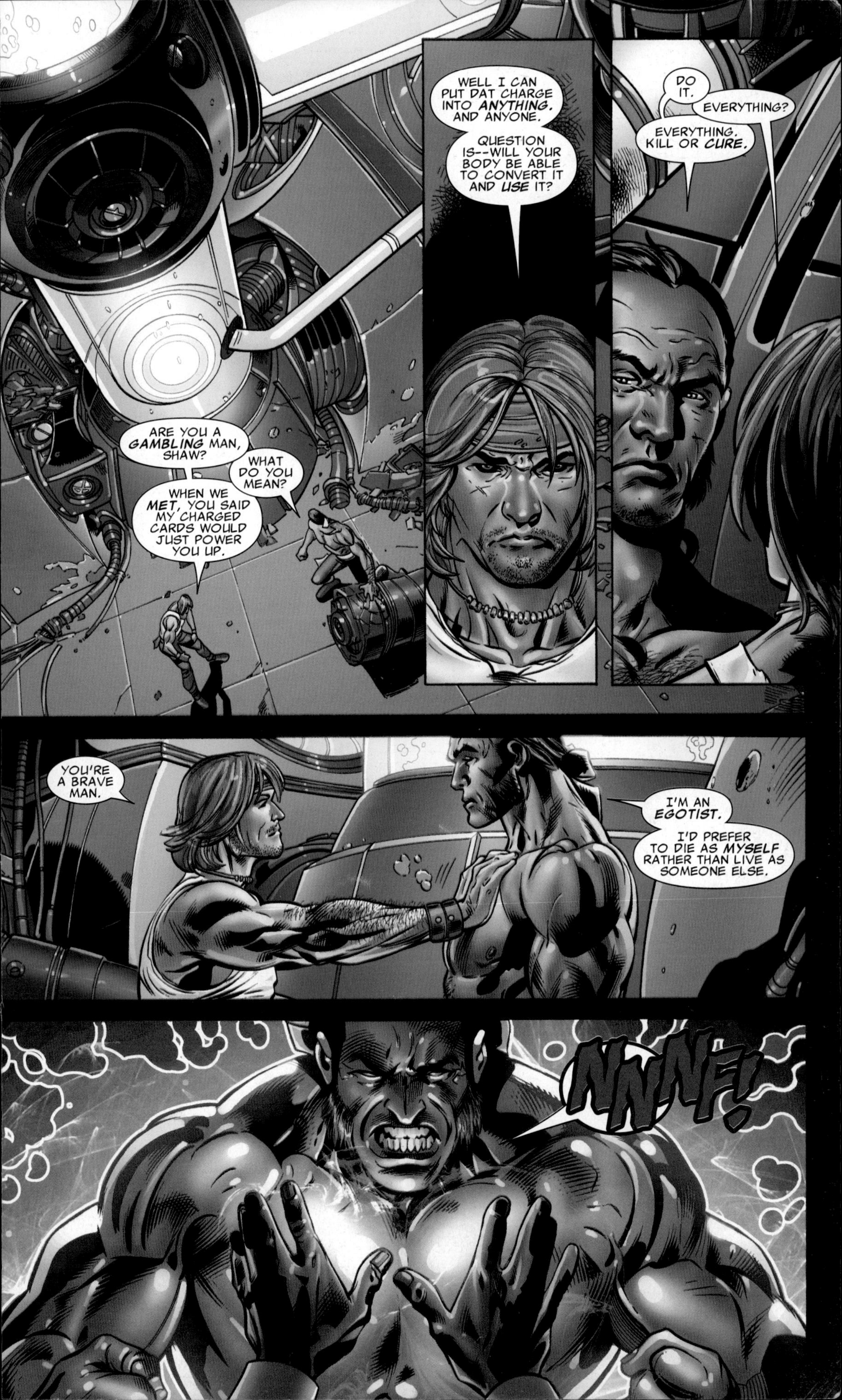

ARE YOU A GAMBLING MAN, SHAW?
WHAT DO YOU MEAN?
WHEN WE MET, YOU SAID MY CHARGED CARDS WOULD JUST POWER YOU UP.
WELL I CAN PUT DAT CHARGE INTO ANYTHING, AND ANYONE.
QUESTION IS--WILL YOUR BODY BE ABLE TO CONVERT IT AND USE IT?
DO IT.
EVERYTHING?
EVERYTHING. KILL OR CURE.
YOU'RE A BRAVE MAN.
I'M AN EGOTIST.
I'D PREFER TO DIE AS MYSELF RATHER THAN LIVE AS SOMEONE ELSE.
NNNF!

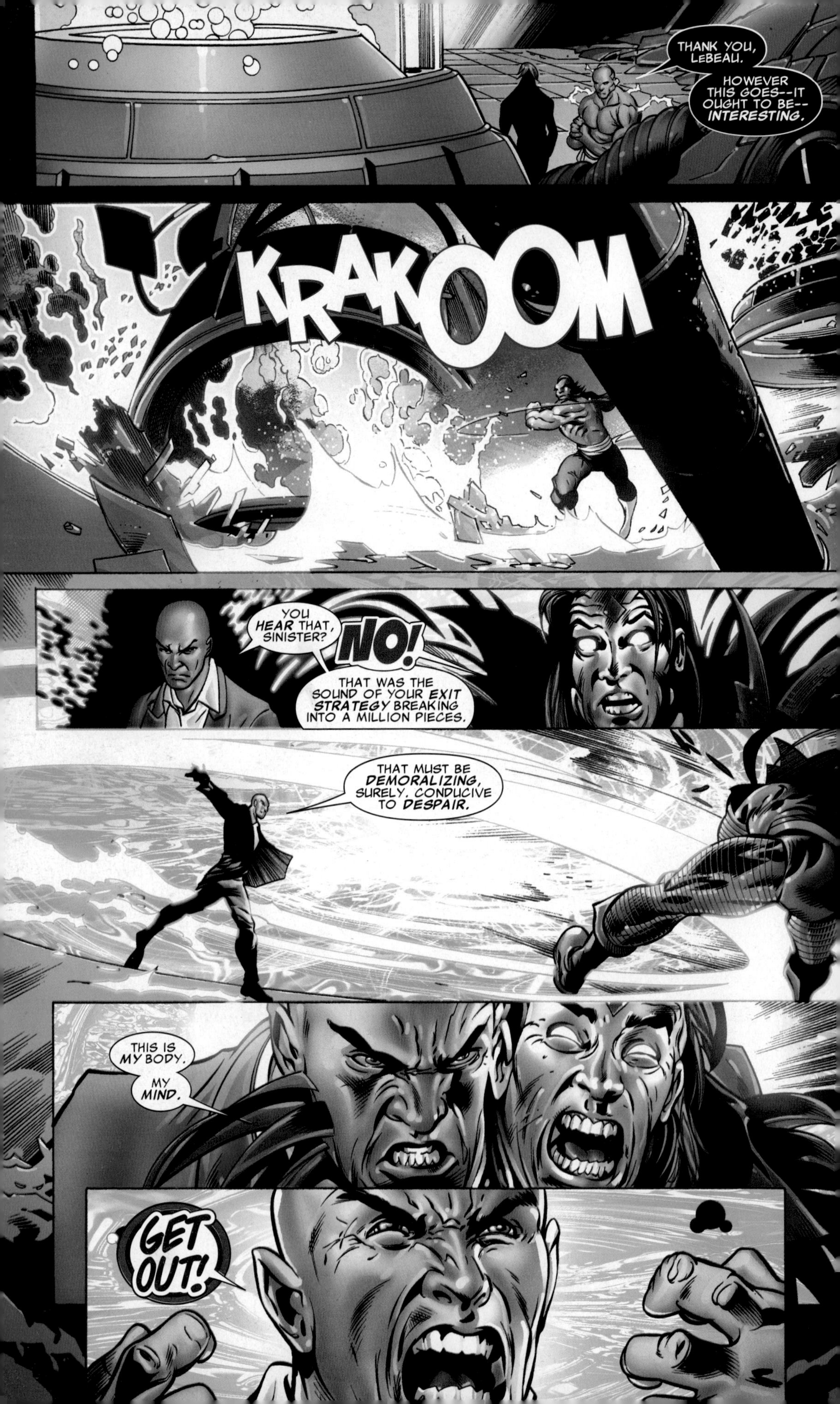

THANK YOU, LEBEAU.
HOWEVER THIS GOES--IT OUGHT TO BE--INTERESTING.
KRAKOOM
YOU HEAR THAT, SINISTER?
NO!
THAT WAS THE SOUND OF YOUR EXIT STRATEGY BREAKING INTO A MILLION PIECES.
THAT MUST BE DEMORALIZING, SURELY. CONDUCIVE TO DESPAIR.
THIS IS MY BODY.
MY MIND.
GET OUT!

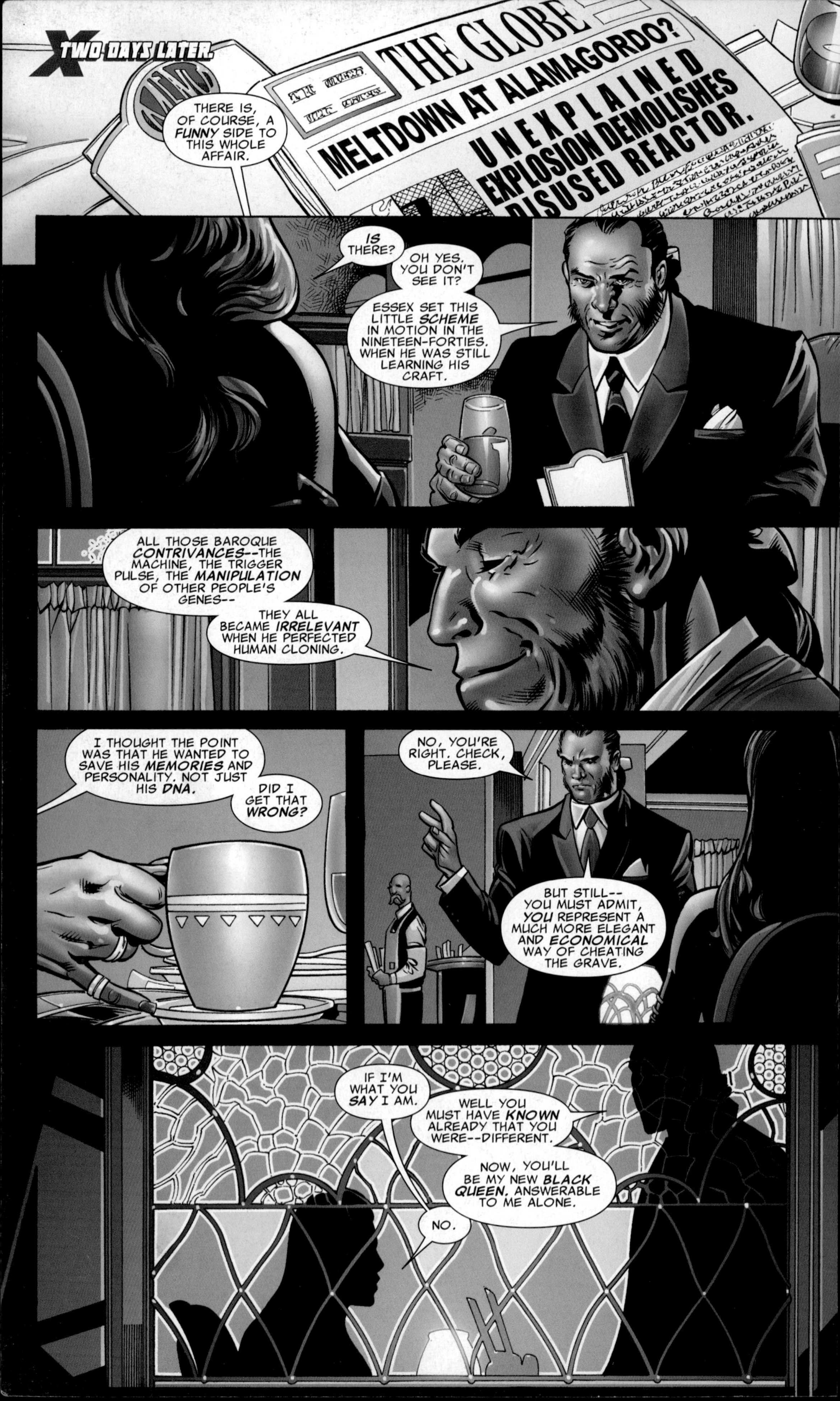

TWO DAYS LATER.
THE GLOBE
MELTDOWN AT ALAMAGORDO?
UNEXPLAINED EXPLOSION DEMOLISHES DISUSED REACTOR.
THERE IS, OF COURSE, A FUNNY SIDE TO THIS WHOLE AFFAIR.
IS THERE?
OH YES. YOU DON'T SEE IT?
ESSEX SET THIS LITTLE SCHEME IN MOTION IN THE NINETEEN-FORTIES. WHEN HE WAS STILL LEARNING HIS CRAFT.
ALL THOSE BAROQUE CONTRIVANCES--THE MACHINE, THE TRIGGER PULSE, THE MANIPULATION OF OTHER PEOPLE'S GENES--
THEY ALL BECAME IRRELEVANT WHEN HE PERFECTED HUMAN CLONING.
I THOUGHT THE POINT WAS THAT HE WANTED TO SAVE HIS MEMORIES AND PERSONALITY. NOT JUST HIS DNA.
DID I GET THAT WRONG?
NO, YOU'RE RIGHT. CHECK, PLEASE.
BUT STILL-- YOU MUST ADMIT, YOU REPRESENT A MUCH MORE ELEGANT AND ECONOMICAL WAY OF CHEATING THE GRAVE.
IF I'M WHAT YOU SAY I AM.
WELL YOU MUST HAVE KNOWN ALREADY THAT YOU WERE--DIFFERENT.
NOW, YOU'LL BE MY NEW BLACK QUEEN. ANSWERABLE TO ME ALONE.
NO.

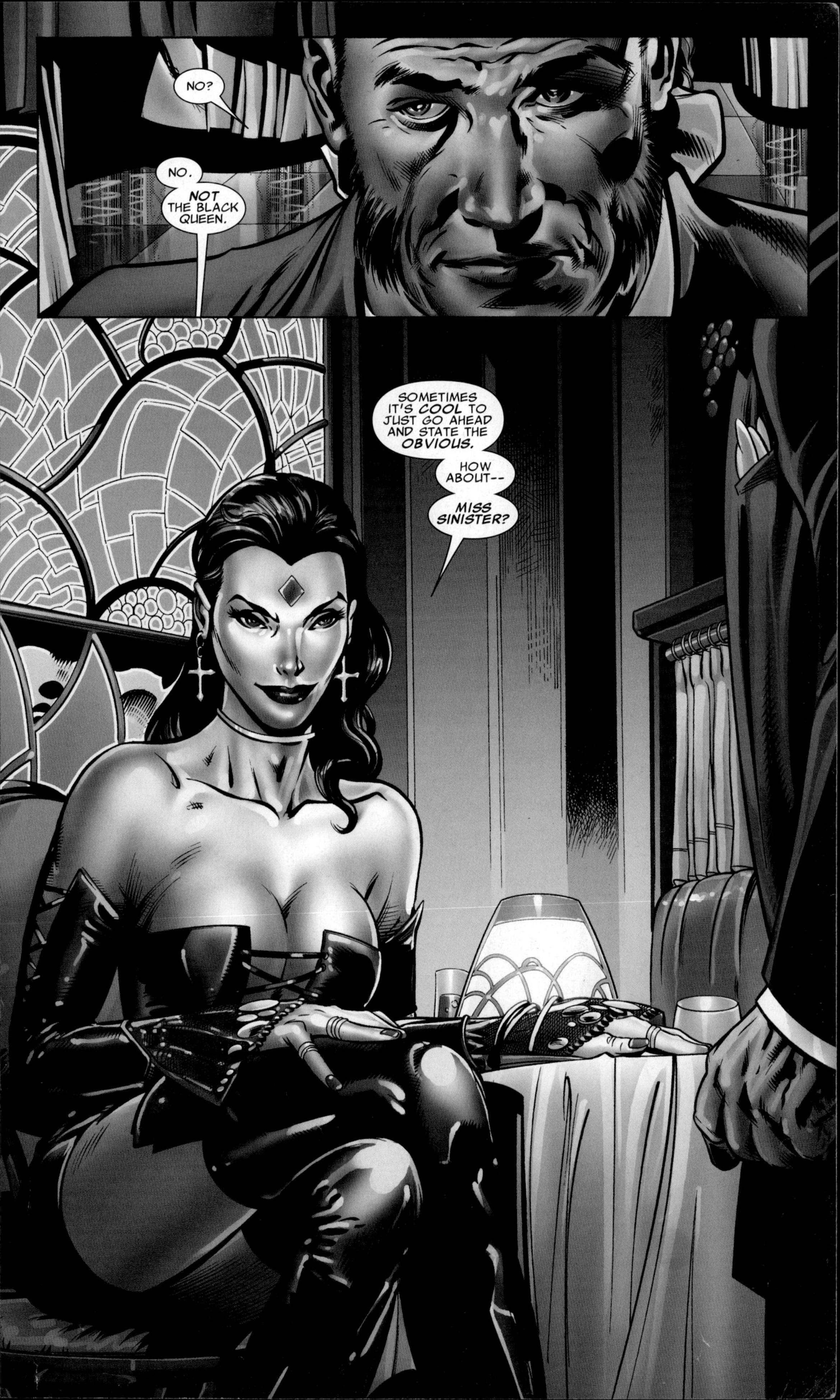
NO?
NO.
NOT THE BLACK QUEEN.
SOMETIMES IT'S COOL TO JUST GO AHEAD AND STATE THE OBVIOUS.
HOW ABOUT--
MISS SINISTER?

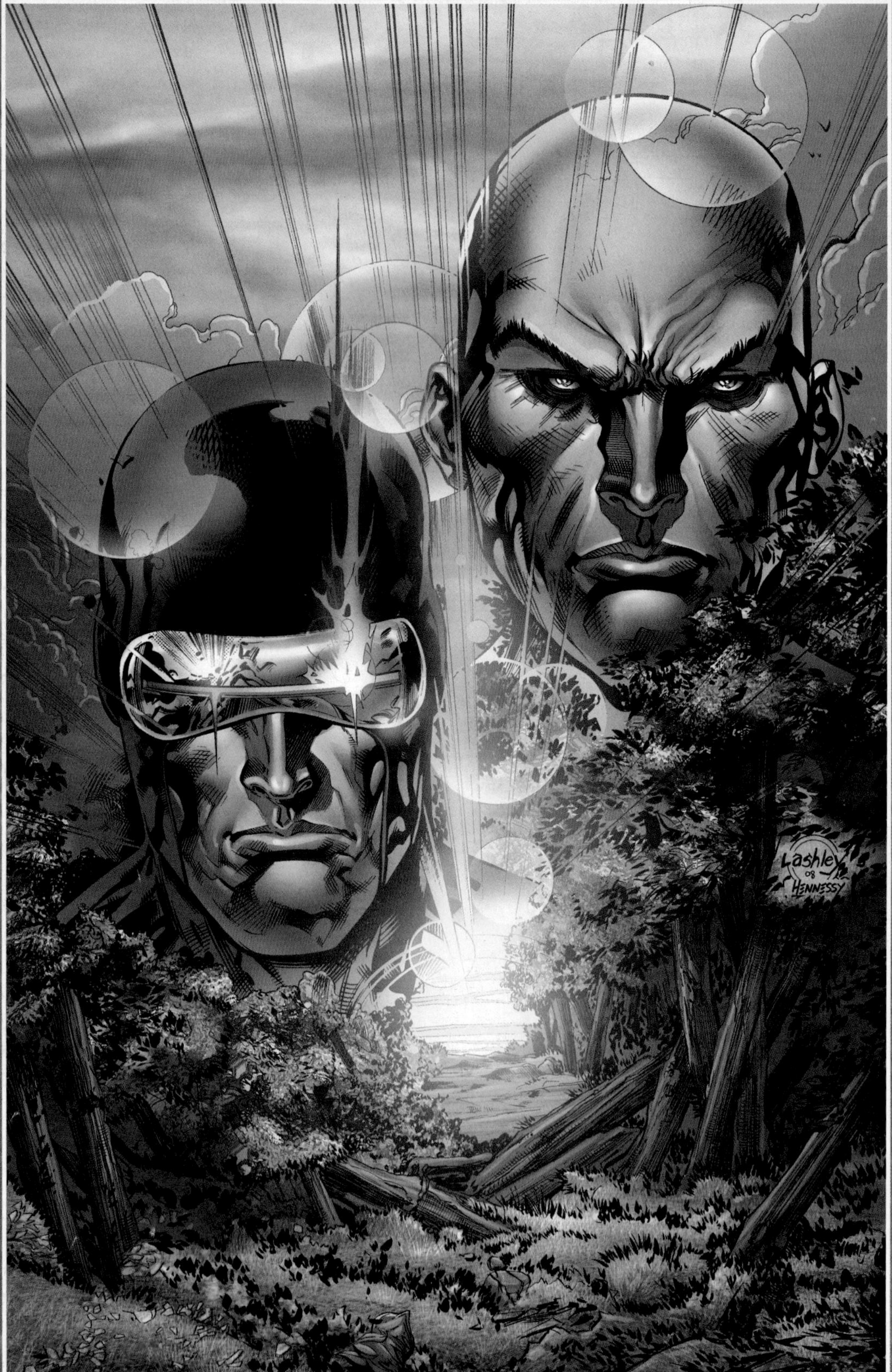
Lashley 08
Hennessy

#215

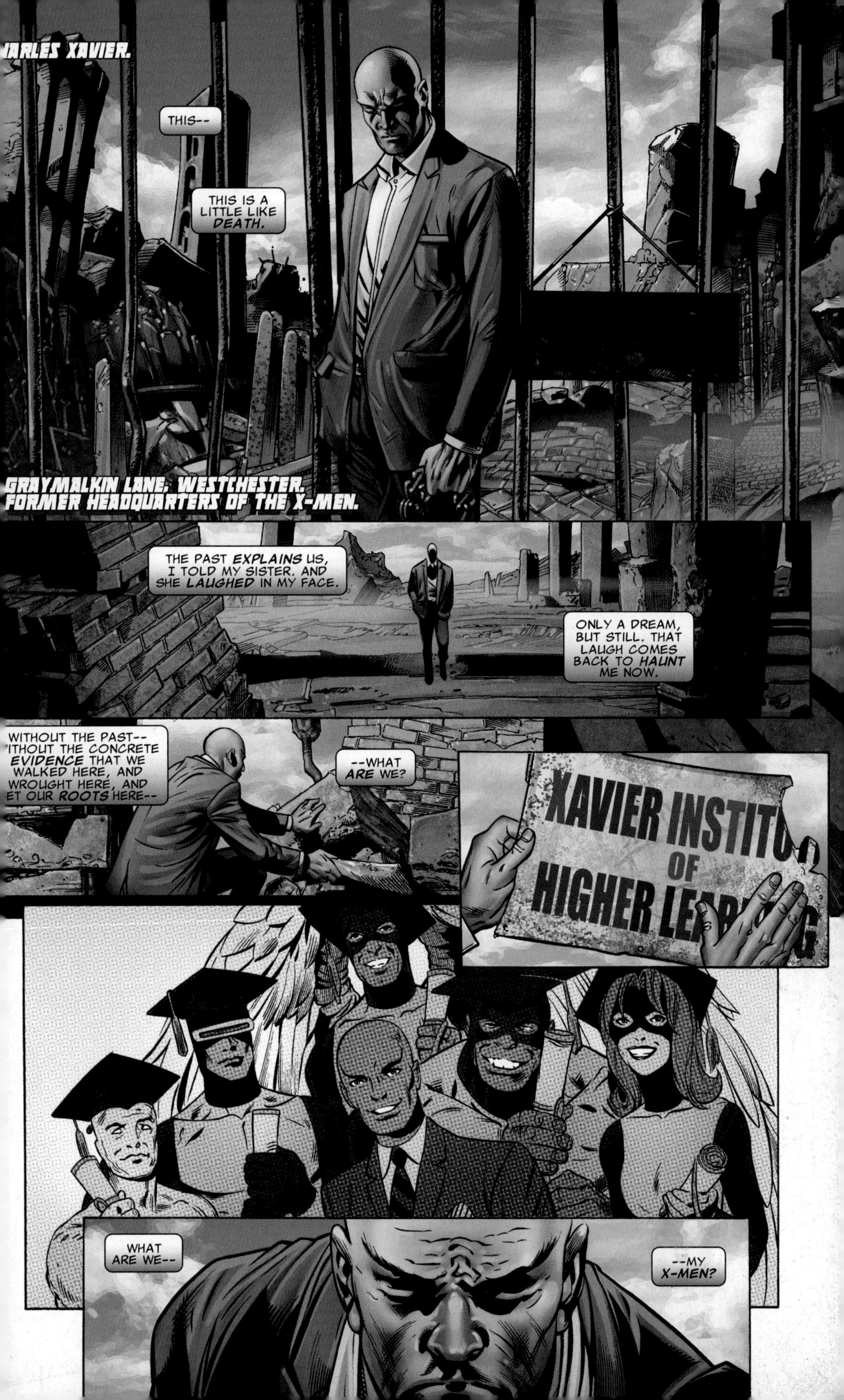
ARLES XAVIER.
THIS--
THIS IS A LITTLE LIKE DEATH.
GRAYMALKIN LANE, WESTCHESTER. FORMER HEADQUARTERS OF THE X-MEN.
THE PAST EXPLAINS US, I TOLD MY SISTER. AND SHE LAUGHED IN MY FACE.
ONLY A DREAM, BUT STILL. THAT LAUGH COMES BACK TO HAUNT ME NOW.
WITHOUT THE PAST-- ITHOUT THE CONCRETE EVIDENCE THAT WE WALKED HERE, AND WROUGHT HERE, AND ET OUR ROOTS HERE--
--WHAT ARE WE?
XAVIER INSTITU OF HIGHER LEA
WHAT ARE WE--
--MY X-MEN?

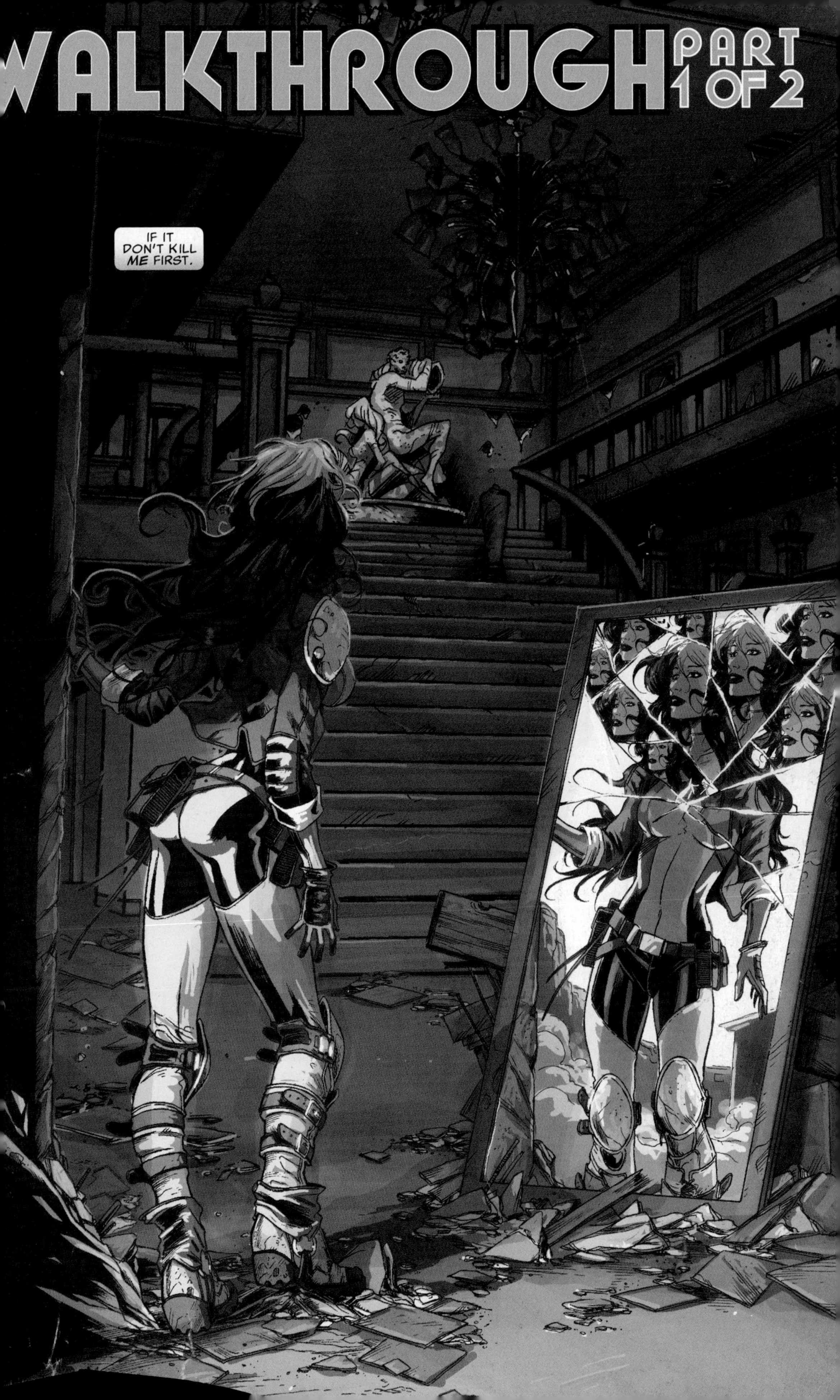
WALKTHROUGH PART 1 OF 2
IF IT DON'T KILL ME FIRST.

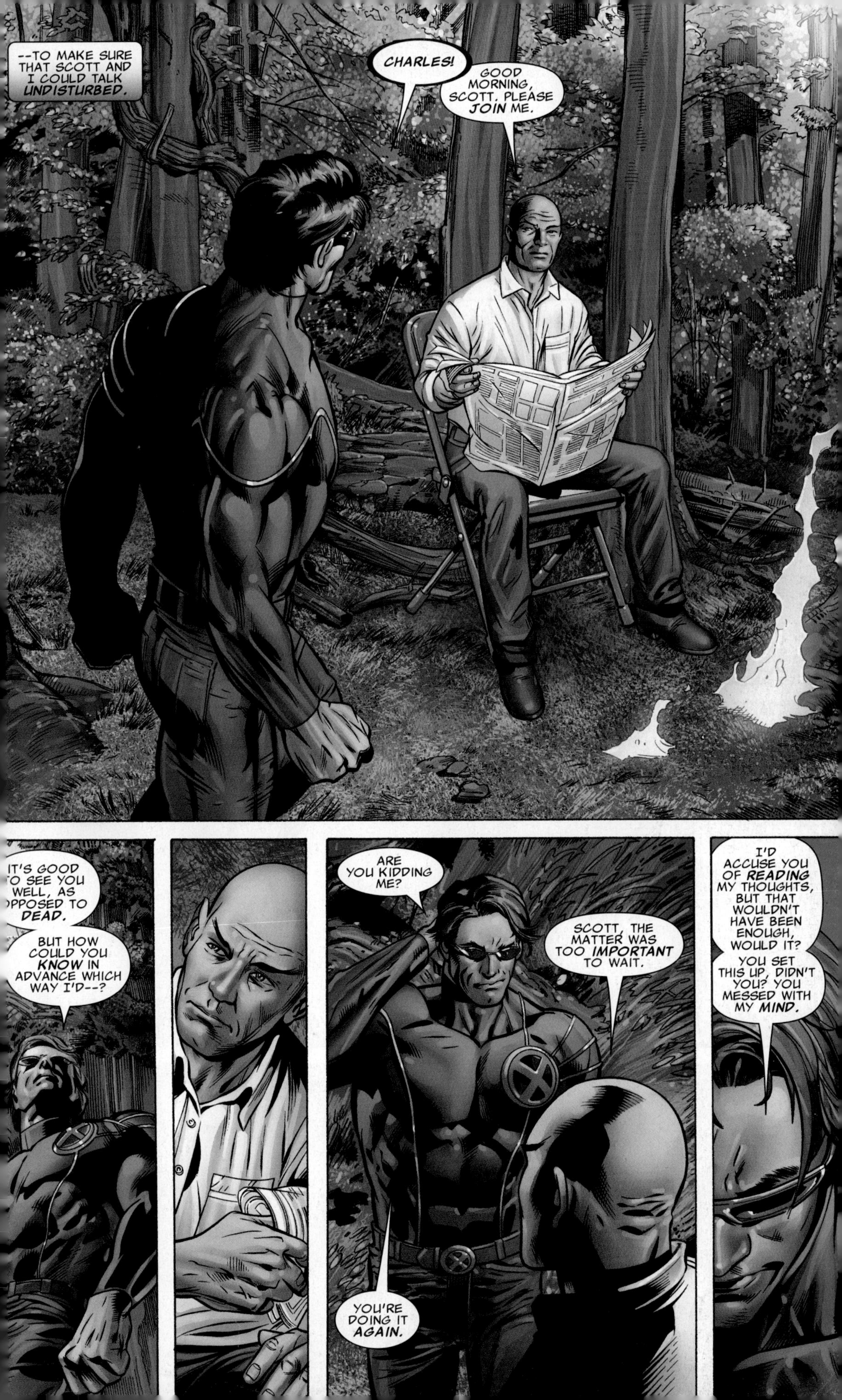
--TO MAKE SURE THAT SCOTT AND I COULD TALK UNDISTURBED.
CHARLES!
GOOD MORNING, SCOTT. PLEASE JOIN ME.
IT'S GOOD TO SEE YOU WELL, AS OPPOSED TO DEAD.
BUT HOW COULD YOU KNOW IN ADVANCE WHICH WAY I'D--?
ARE YOU KIDDING ME?
SCOTT, THE MATTER WAS TOO IMPORTANT TO WAIT.
YOU'RE DOING IT AGAIN.
I'D ACCUSE YOU OF READING MY THOUGHTS, BUT THAT WOULDN'T HAVE BEEN ENOUGH, WOULD IT?
YOU SET THIS UP, DIDN'T YOU? YOU MESSED WITH MY MIND.

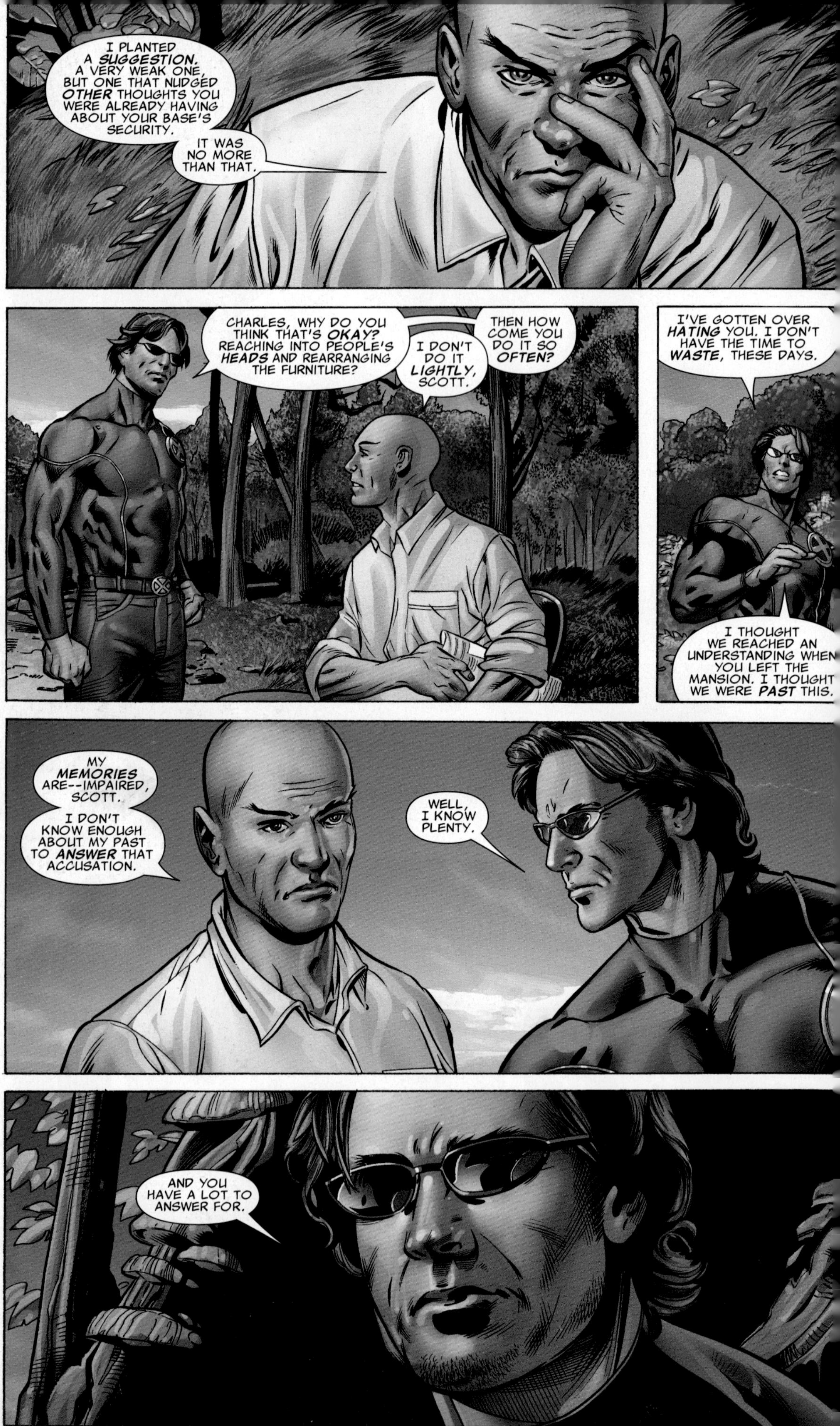
I PLANTED A SUGGESTION. A VERY WEAK ONE, BUT ONE THAT NUDGED OTHER THOUGHTS YOU WERE ALREADY HAVING ABOUT YOUR BASE'S SECURITY.
IT WAS NO MORE THAN THAT.
CHARLES, WHY DO YOU THINK THAT'S OKAY? REACHING INTO PEOPLE'S HEADS AND REARRANGING THE FURNITURE?
I DON'T DO IT LIGHTLY, SCOTT.
THEN HOW COME YOU DO IT SO OFTEN?
I'VE GOTTEN OVER HATING YOU. I DON'T HAVE THE TIME TO WASTE, THESE DAYS.
I THOUGHT WE REACHED AN UNDERSTANDING WHEN YOU LEFT THE MANSION. I THOUGHT WE WERE PAST THIS.
MY MEMORIES ARE--IMPAIRED, SCOTT.
I DON'T KNOW ENOUGH ABOUT MY PAST TO ANSWER THAT ACCUSATION.
WELL, I KNOW PLENTY.
AND YOU HAVE A LOT TO ANSWER FOR.

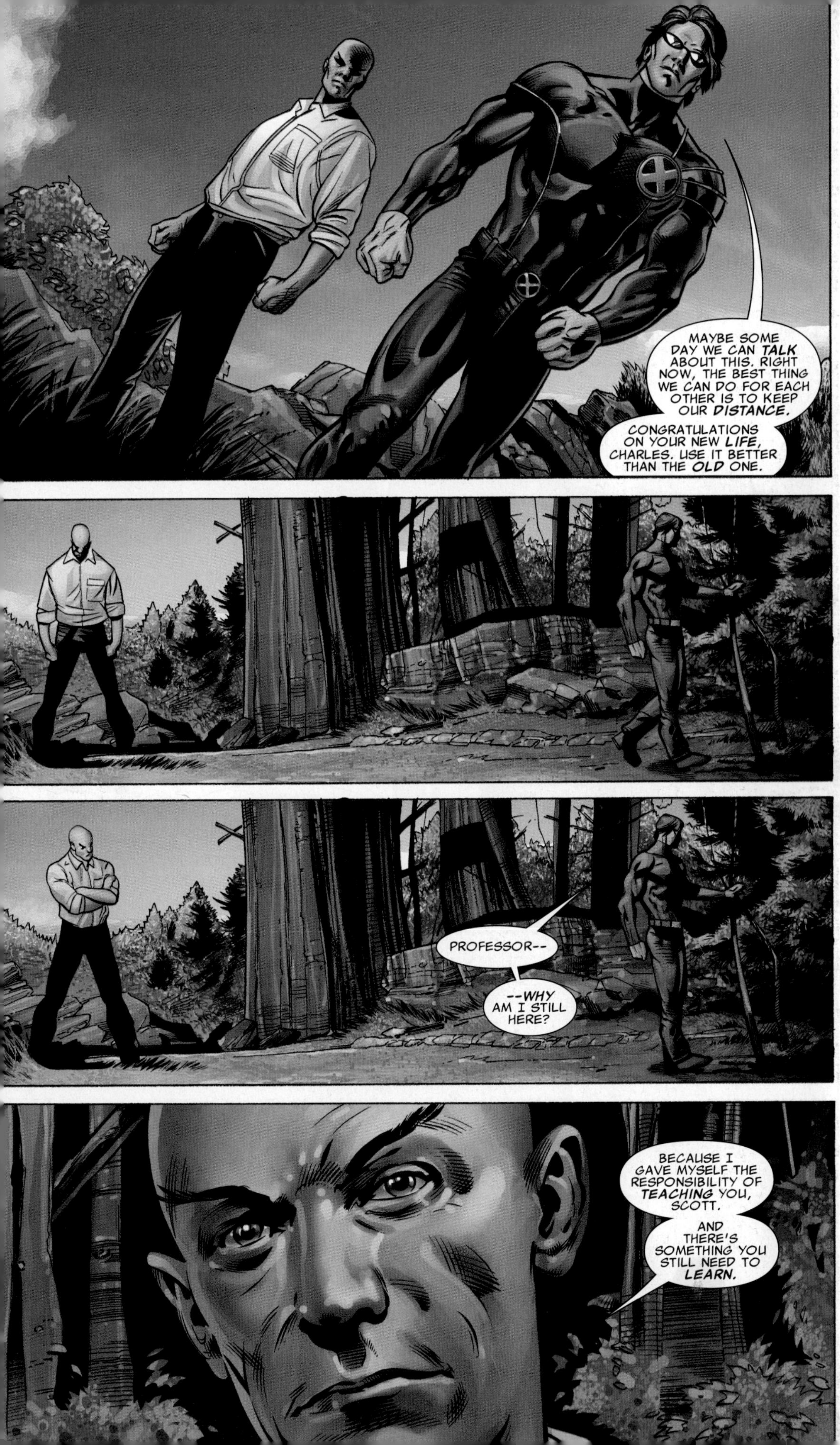
MAYBE SOME DAY WE CAN TALK ABOUT THIS. RIGHT NOW, THE BEST THING WE CAN DO FOR EACH OTHER IS TO KEEP OUR DISTANCE.
CONGRATULATIONS ON YOUR NEW LIFE, CHARLES. USE IT BETTER THAN THE OLD ONE.
PROFESSOR--
--WHY AM I STILL HERE?
BECAUSE I GAVE MYSELF THE RESPONSIBILITY OF TEACHING YOU, SCOTT.
AND THERE'S SOMETHING YOU STILL NEED TO LEARN.

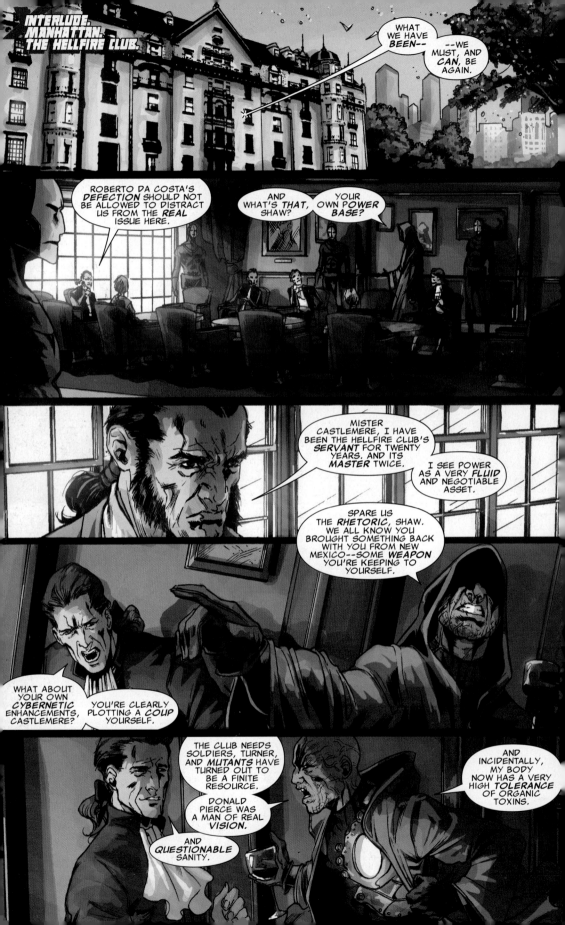

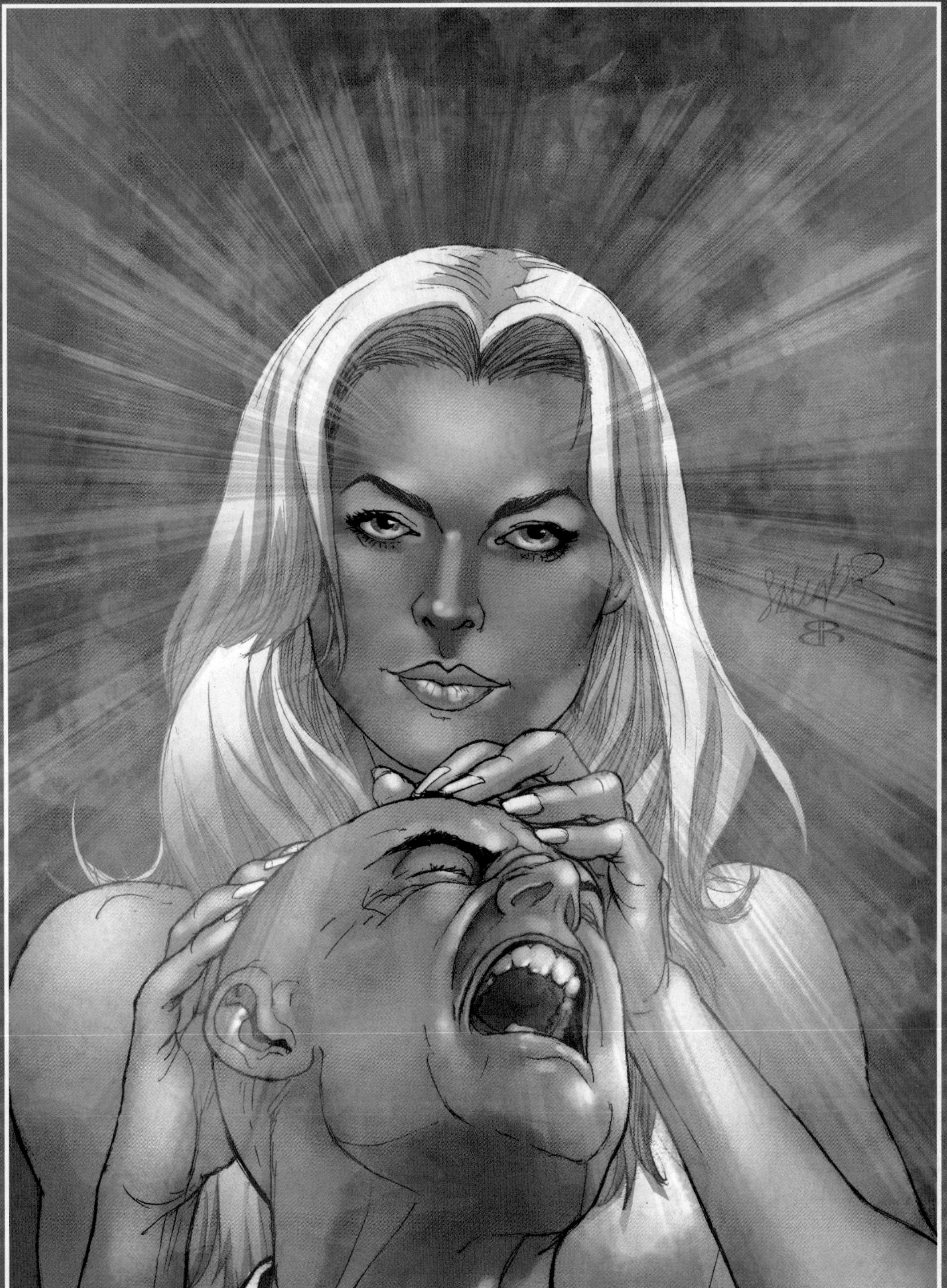

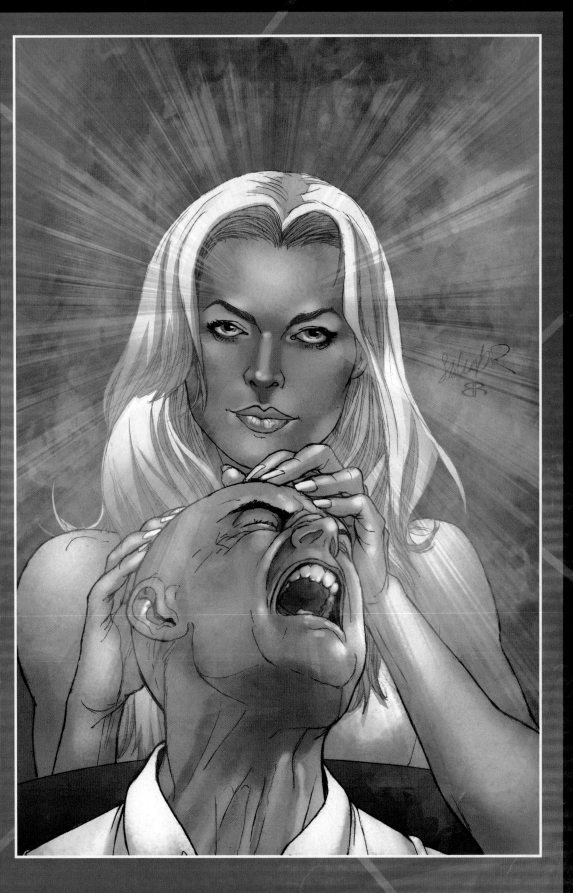

#216

"BUT I THINK THERE ARE SOME SCENES COMING UP THAT I'LL WANT TO LOOK *AWAY* FROM."

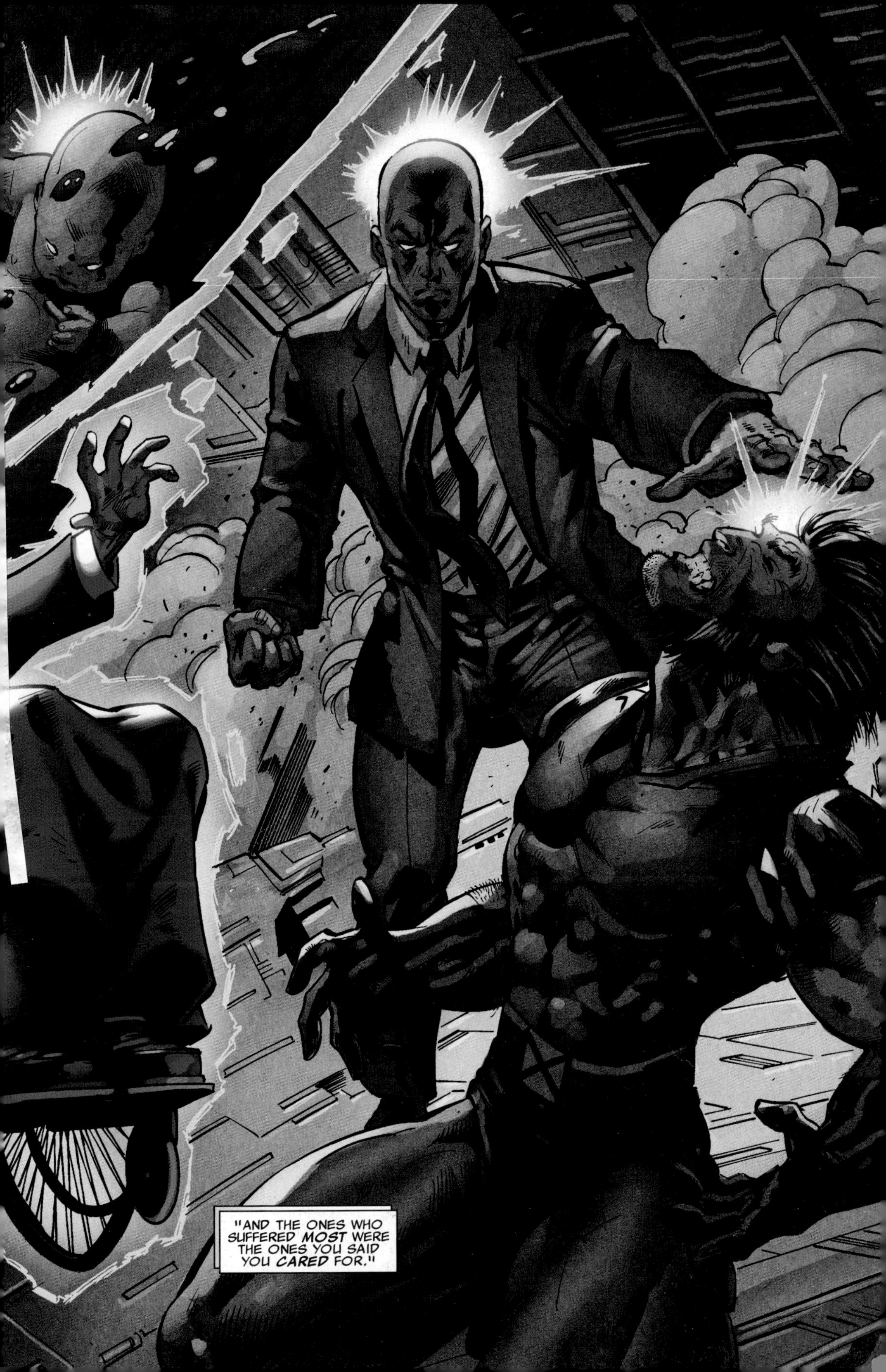
"AND THE ONES WHO SUFFERED MOST WERE THE ONES YOU SAID YOU CARED FOR."

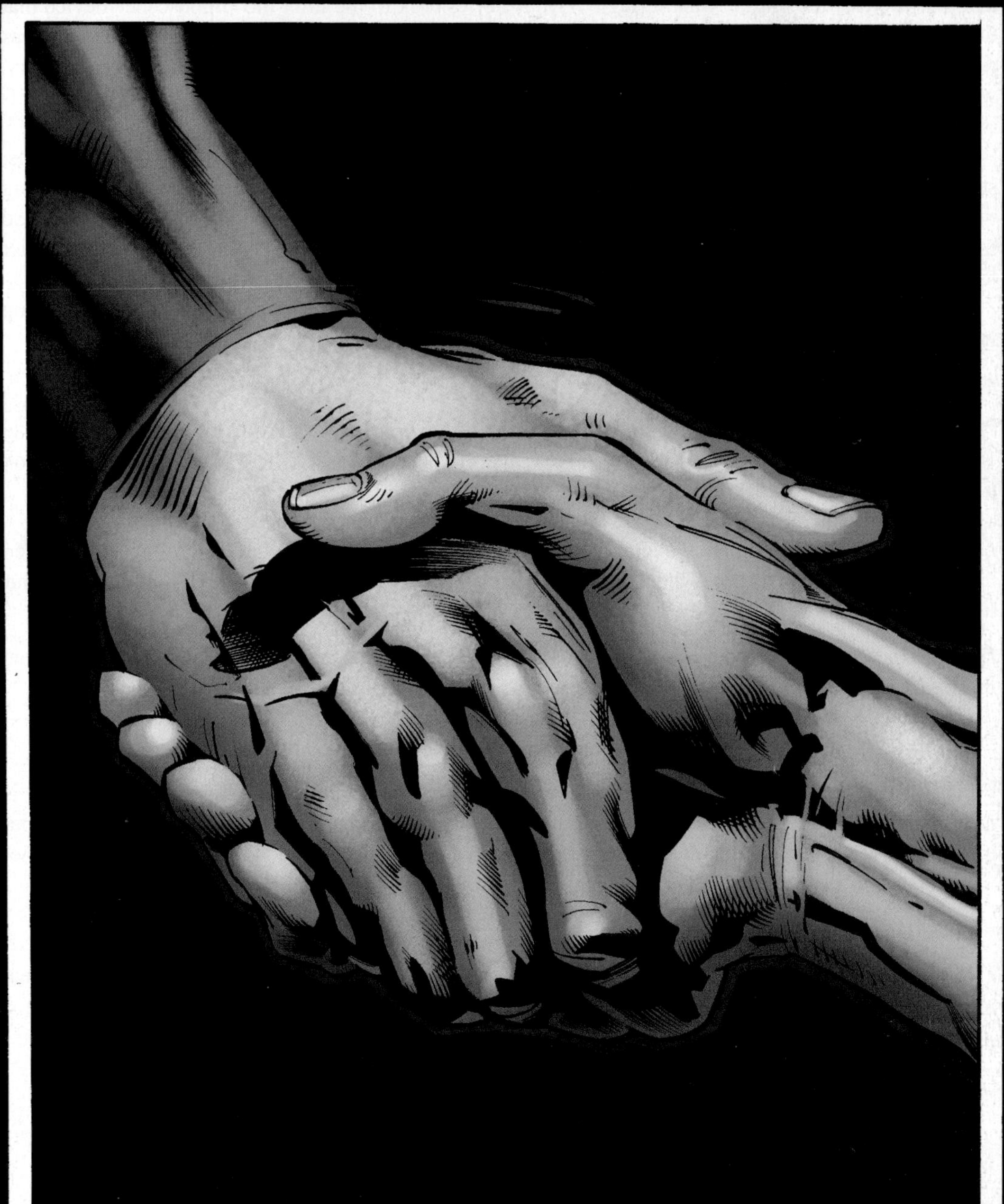
NEXT:
ORIGINAL SIN

THE MINDSCAPE PAPERS

The book you're reading covers the climax of the second Legacy storyline, "Sins of the Father", and the whole of the third, "Walkthrough". Both stories took to the limit the "mindscape" device that we'd been using to define Professor Xavier's quest on the page, to illustrate the way in which he was re-experiencing the memories of his past life as he recovered them. Each issue was basically a tapestry, weaving through a great deal of past X-Men continuity and tying it to the theme of Professor X's self-examination: his attempt to understand his own past actions and motivations.

When I was writing these issues, I had to layer in a lot of references to a lot of different X-Men stories, stretching back over four decades. Obviously this was a labour of love, in a lot of ways: I was choosing moments that had been significant in the life of Professor X, but I was also going for stories that had meant something to me as a reader. It's an armchair anthology of the stories that brought Charles Xavier to the fore as the creator and leader of the X-Men: his greatest hours, his blood and sweat and tears.

For completists, these notes comprise a list of the stories we referenced. If I've missed out something important, remember that I caught a ricochet from Bishop's bullet.

#213, SINS OF THE FATHER PART 3

P6&7: "I ordered Jean's silence…" This first scene is from *Uncanny #65*. Professor X was playing dead while he figured out a way to defeat the Z'Nox, and this was the issue where Marvel Girl and Havok spilled the beans to the rest of the team.

The second sequence ("Professor, can I talk to you?") is from the early heyday of the Claremont era — *Uncanny #129*. It's a fascinating example of how differently Professor Xavier and Cyclops approached the training and management of the new X-Men team. I can't read this page without thinking of Arthur Miller's *All My Sons*.

P10: "He took out part of your brain…" The origin of Gambit's association with Sinister, as portrayed in *Gambit* (3rd series) *#14*.

For Jacob Shaw's involvement with Mister Sinister, see the *X-Men: Hellfire Club* miniseries — especially #3. I don't think we ever learned until now what Sinister got out of that deal.

P13: Amanda Mueller's involvement in the Alamogordo project and her alliance with Sinister is documented in *X-Men Forever #4*. The visual of her sitting in the dark like a withered, ageless spider in a digital web, manipulating events from a distance, was one that stayed with me. Thank (or blame) Fabian Nicieza and penciler Kevin Maguire.

#214: SINS OF THE FATHER, PART 4

P1: Professor X originally gave this speech way, way, way back in *Uncanny #1*. He didn't repeat himself back then, though.

P7: This lovely splash brings together images from a whole lot of different places:

- Child Xavier being thrashed by Kurt Marko
- The hate-crime beating that almost killed Xavier in *UXM #192*
- Xavier's heart attack from *UXM #200*
- The shattering of Xavier's spine (second time around) in the Muir Island Saga
- Xavier on the cross from "Eve of Destruction"
- Xavier dying in Hank's arms in *XM #120* (I know, I know, it's actually Xavier's mind in Cassandra Nova's body.)
- Xavier being shot in the head by Bishop in the "Messiah Complex" Crossover

P10: Xavier took a bullet from Stryfe in *Uncanny #294*, the issue that launched The "X-Cutioner's Song". The bullet infected the Professor with the techno-organic virus, and there was all sorts of hell to pay.

P13: The reference here is to *Uncanny #167*, when the Brood queen that had been incubating in the Professor's body from the start of his relationship with the New Mutants finally hatched out. That was also the issue in which the X-Men came back to Earth after their own traumatic encounter with the Brood. Happy days.

P15: Xavier as Onslaught. Hmm. Not so happy days, for a reader of my era, but it had to be there.

#215: WALKTHROUGH, PART 1

P1: "I told my sister…" He did, but it was in another mindscape sequence, in *Legacy #211*, not in reality. The graduation photo is a reference to the events of *Uncanny #7*.

P2: "Maynards Plains". Okay, I just flat-out made that up. The X-Men took over the Reavers' ghost town HQ in *Uncanny #229*, but I couldn't find a single issue in which it was ever given a name.

The Rogue/Colossus scene takes place in *Uncanny #231*. I loved those playful moments when they came. It's amazing how seldom I write them, though.

P13: For young Scott Summers' exploits at the Nebraska orphanage, and for his relationship with Lefty, see *Classic X-Men #41*.

The image of Mister Sinister observing a ten-year-old Jean Grey isn't a specific flashback: it's just something I think we can assume to have happened, given his obsessive nature and what we know of his interest in her bloodline.

P16: This very poignant scene is in canon: I got it from *Uncanny #244*. I loved the tortured, twisted interplay between Rogue and Carol Danvers, and around about this time it was getting particularly fascinating.

#216: WALKTHROUGH, PART 2

P4: The first place where the story of Beast's joining the X-Men was told was as a back-up story in *Uncanny*, issues *#49-53*. I retold it recently in an *X-Men: Origins* book: this beat – Professor X erasing Hank McCoy from living memory – still amazes me. Okay, it was dreamed up in a more innocent age, but as an illustration of the sheer brute-force scale of Professor X's powers, this is the supreme example.

P7: The story I'm referencing here is in *Uncanny #171*. We see Rogue arriving at the mansion, and we see Professor X taking her away to his study for a one-to-one conversation. The content of that conversation was never revealed before this issue.

P11: Referencing the events of *Deadly Genesis #6*, although again we're seeing what happened between the moments that we saw there.

P13&14: The spread here is built around the theme of the most questionable and disturbing things that Professor X has done over the years. Xavier mind-wiping Magneto (from "Fatal Attractions" – *X-Men #25*) takes pride of place. Alongside this, we have:

- Xavier fighting Cassandra Nova in the womb.
- Xavier and the X-Men confronting Danger in the Savage Land, from the second Astonishing arc.
- Xavier stopping Amelia Voght from leaving him (only momentarily, but still…) from *UXM #309*.
- A non-canonical scene, teasing the events of "Original Sin" – Wolverine in classic yellow and black costume kneels at Xavier's feet, head thrown back, screaming to the skies, as Xavier stands over him, one hand raised, and works on his mind: brain surgery without a scalpel or anaesthetic.

P17: "Listen well to those who love you". To see this sequence, and the death of Moira MacTaggert, in its full narrative context, you should (you really should) obtain and read *X-Men #108*. It's part of the Muir Island Saga (well, "Dreams End") so it's got to have been reprinted somewhere.* Okay, you either get a lump in your throat at Moira's death or you don't, but I defy you not to be moved by the Xavier/Jean stuff.

P21: "Jean told me…" As with the Xavier-Cassandra dialogue, don't give yourself a nose-bleed looking for this one. I made it up, and put it into *Legacy #211*.

And that's it. In case I didn't say this already, writing this book draws a zig-zag line through so much of my own childhood that I almost feel it's my mind we're walking through. My big brother Chris gave me my first X-Men comic, and tore me off a strip because I creased the cover. I was seven years old, and kids still cleaned chimneys or went to work in mines.

My job is better.

—Mike Carey, *October 2008*

---

*It's reprinted in *X-Men: Dream's End!* On sale now! —Jen "Trade Monger" Grünwald

ALAN DAVIS COVER PROCESS

ISSUE #213 SKETCHES

ISSUE #214 SKETCHES

ISSUE #213 PENCILS   **ISSUE #214 PENCILS**

ISSUE #213 INKS

ISSUE #214 INKS

MISS SINISTER CHARACTER SKETCHES BY SCOT EATON

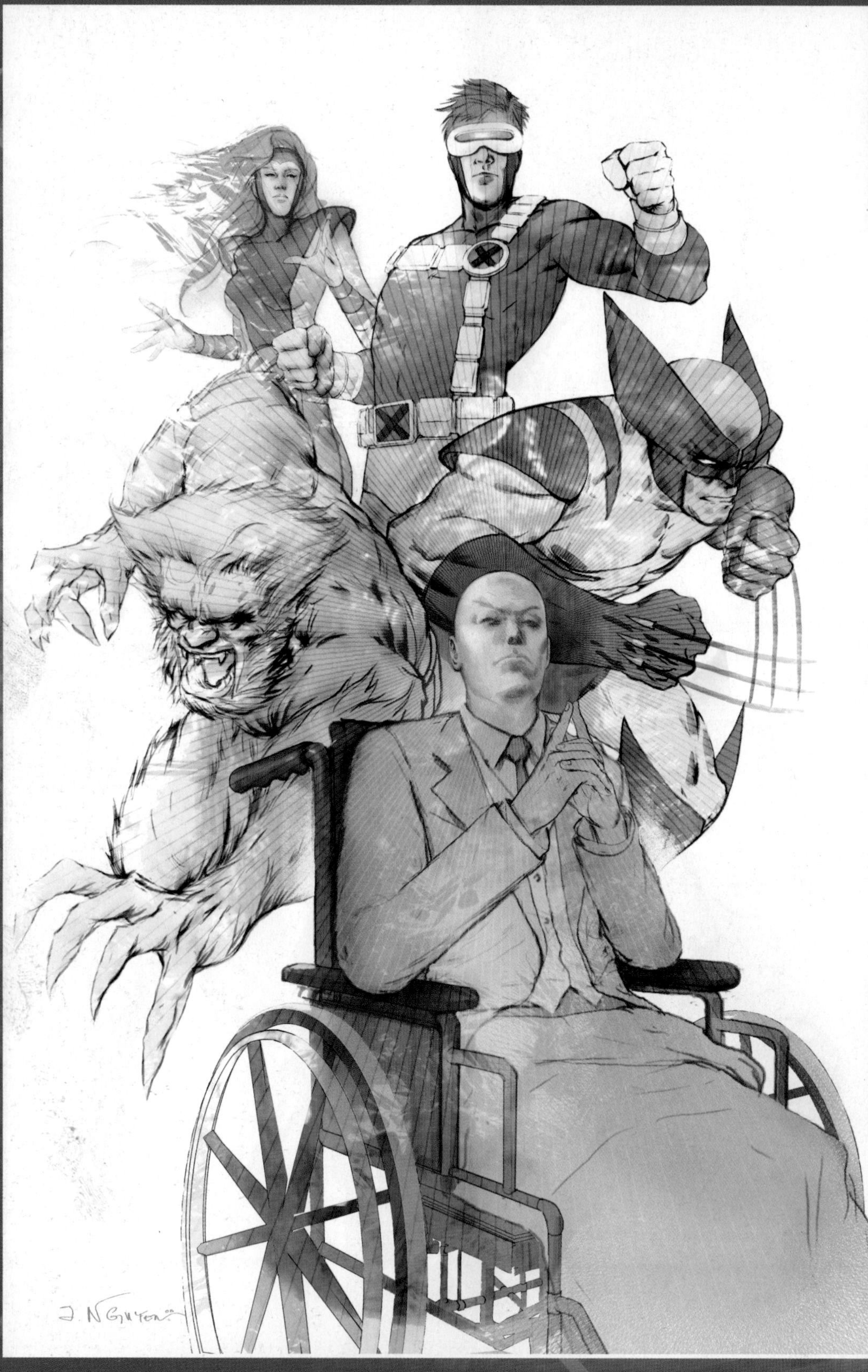
J. NGUYEN

X-MEN: ODD MEN OUT

JEAN? REPORT.

NOTHING SUSPICIOUS WITHIN A FIVE MILE RADIUS, PROFESSOR.

VERY GOOD. MAINTAIN AERIAL SURVEILLANCE AND INFORM ME IF THE SITUATION CHANGES...

"...WE'RE GOING IN."

HELLO, CHARLES! IT'S GOOD TO SEE YOU AGAIN... IN THE FLESH, I MEAN.

GOOD EVENING, FRED.

AND... HANK MCCOY, ISN'T IT?

YES, SIR. IT'S BEEN A LONG TIME.

UH, EXCUSE ME, BUT I THOUGHT THAT YOU...

...HAD ONCE AGAIN BECOME HIRSUTE? ALAS, 'TIS TRUE! THE BEARDLESS YOUTH I ONCE WAS IS NOW LITTLE MORE THAN TREASURED REMEMBRANCE...

...ONLY OCCASIONALLY RESURRECTED, LIKE SOME GHOSTLY SHADE, VIA THIS MIRACULOUS, MICROCIRCUITED IMAGE-INDUCER.

A CONVENIENT BIT OF CAMOUFLAGE, NO?

BUT ENOUGH ELUCIDATION... I'LL LEAVE YOU TWO TO YOUR OWN DEVICES AND JOIN THE OTHERS IN THE FIELD!

THANK YOU, HENRY.

OTHERS? FIELD?!

"...AS I RECALL, I HAD LEARNED THAT YOU HAD BEEN NAMED TO HEAD THE BUREAU'S INVESTIGATION OF MUTANT ACTIVITIES..."

WHY THE LONG FACE, FRED? THIS "MUTANT MENACE" THING SOUNDS LIKE A PLUM ASSIGNMENT!

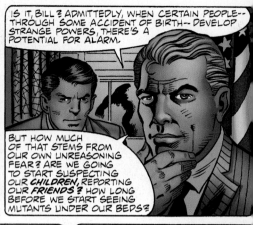

IS IT, BILL? ADMITTEDLY, WHEN CERTAIN PEOPLE--THROUGH SOME ACCIDENT OF BIRTH--DEVELOP STRANGE POWERS, THERE'S A POTENTIAL FOR ALARM.

BUT HOW MUCH OF THAT STEMS FROM OUR OWN UNREASONING FEAR? ARE WE GOING TO START SUSPECTING OUR CHILDREN, REPORTING OUR FRIENDS? HOW LONG BEFORE WE START SEEING MUTANTS UNDER OUR BEDS?

"IN RETROSPECT, I SHOULD HAVE FOUND A BETTER WAY OF REVEALING MY PRESENCE..."

?!? HOW IN BLAZES DID YOU GET IN HERE? THIS IS A HIGH SECURITY AREA!

WELL, I DON'T KNOW HOW HE GOT IN... BUT I KNOW HOW HE'S GOING OUT!

-UNNHH!- WHAT IS THIS!? I CAN'T BUDGE HIM!

YOU MERELY THINK YOU ARE PUSHING WITH ALL YOUR MIGHT!

IN REALITY, IT IS YOU WHO ARE IMMOBILIZED, BY ME!

YOU? THEN YOU'RE A MUTANT... SET ON STOPPING OUR INVESTIGATION?

I AM A MUTANT BUT, I ASSURE YOU, THAT'S NOT MY PURPOSE. THERE'S NO NEED FOR THAT GUN... YOU'LL FIND THAT YOU CANNOT EVEN SQUEEZE THE TRIGGER!

I APOLOGIZE FOR THE RATHER MELODRAMATIC DEMONSTRATION OF MY MENTAL POWERS, BUT NOW PERHAPS YOU'LL ALLOW ME TO EXPLAIN WHO I AM... AND WHY I'M HERE! I PROPOSE TO HELP YOU--

--TO HELP US ALL -- BY PERSONALLY LOCATING AND CONTACTING THIS NATION'S MUTANT MINORITY.

IF THEY ARE HOUNDED--PERSECUTED--THEY MIGHT BECOME THE VERY MENACE HUMANITY FEARS! BUT IF I CAN PROVIDE THEM WITH A PROPER OUTLET FOR THEIR POWERS--!

"I WAS VERY LUCKY THAT DAY. I'D FOUND THE RIGHT MAN TO SUPPORT MY PLAN..."

ALL RIGHT, PROFESSOR, I'LL SUPPLY YOU WITH DATA... AND YOU'LL REPORT PERIODICALLY TO ME!

LET US HOPE WE HAVE BOTH REASONED CORRECTLY, DUNCAN, THE SURVIVAL OF CIVILIZATION MAY DEPEND UPON IT.

"THE MONTHS WHICH FOLLOWED WERE BUSY ONES. I BEGAN RECRUITING STUDENTS FOR MY **SCHOOL FOR GIFTED YOUNGSTERS**--

"--AND THE PUBLIC NEVER KNEW JUST HOW 'GIFTED' THOSE YOUNGSTERS WERE--

"--OR REALIZED THAT MY ACADEMY WAS TRAINING THE FIRST FIVE **X-MEN**!

"HOW I REMEMBER THOSE EARLY TRAINING SESSIONS!

"WARREN WORTHINGTON TRULY CAME ALIVE AS THE **ANGEL**, HAPPY THAT HE NO LONGER HAD TO KEEP HIS WINGS HIDDEN--

"--AND HENRY MCCOY RELISHED THE OPPORTUNITY TO TEST HIS **BEAST**-LIKE STRENGTH AND AGILITY.

"SCOTT SUMMERS, THE OLDEST AND MOST RESERVED OF MY FIRST CLASS, WORKED TO CONTAIN HIS POWERFUL EYE-BEAMS BEHIND THE VISOR OF THE **CYCLOPS**.

"WHILE YOUNG BOBBY DRAKE DILIGENTLY REFINED HIS MASTERY OF TEMPERATURES AS THE **ICEMAN**.

"THE PSYCHO-KINETIC JEAN GREY WAS THE LAST TO OFFICIALLY JOIN THAT FIRST TEAM.

"--FROM THE MUTANT WHO WOULD BECOME OUR DEADLIEST FOE...

"I'M SORRY NOW THAT I DIDN'T COME UP WITH A BETTER CODE-NAME FOR HER THAN **MARVEL GIRL**, BUT I HAD LITTLE TIME TO RECONSIDER THEN. SHE HAD JUST JOINED US, WHEN WE FACED OUR FIRST THREAT--

"...**MAGNETO**, MASTER OF MAGNETISM!

"MY X-MEN ENDED HIS OCCUPATION OF THE **CAPE CITADEL** MISSILE BASE--

"--BUT MAGNETO RETURNED AGAIN AND AGAIN...

"...GATHERING MASTER-MIND, QUICKSILVER AND THE SCARLET WITCH, AND THE TOAD INTO A MUTANT BROTHERHOOD TO OPPOSE US.

"THEY WERE OUR GREATEST ENEMIES IN THAT EARLY PERIOD, BUT THEY BY NO MEANS POSED THE ONLY DANGER.

"WE FACED THREATS FROM OTHER MUTANTS... THE BLOB, THE VANISHER, LINUS THE UN-TOUCHABLE, EVEN THE LEGENDARY SUB-MARINER...

...AS WELL AS FROM OTHER SOURCES, LIKE MY OLD ENEMY LUCIFER.

A DANGEROUS BUNCH, EVERY ONE OF THEM!

YOU CAN BE PROUD, CHARLES. YOUR KIDS FACED SOME OF THE TOUGHEST OPPONENTS THAT EVER WALKED THE EARTH--AND **WON** EVERY TIME!

NOT **EVERY** TIME, FRED. THEY NEVER TOTALLY OVERCAME MAGNETO.

MAYBE NOT, BUT THEY ALWAYS MANAGED TO SAVE THE DAY.

YOU TRAINED THEM SO WELL THAT THEY WERE EVEN ABLE TO GET ALONG WITHOUT YOU. I'LL NEVER FORGET THAT TIME...

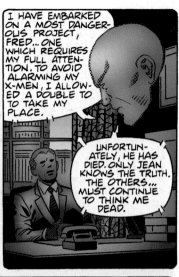

I HAVE EMBARKED ON A MOST DANGER-OUS PROJECT, FRED... ONE WHICH REQUIRES MY FULL ATTEN-TION. TO AVOID ALARMING MY X-MEN, I ALLOW-ED A DOUBLE TO TAKE MY PLACE.

UNFORTUN-ATELY, HE HAS DIED. ONLY JEAN KNOWS THE TRUTH. THE OTHERS... MUST CONTINUE TO THINK ME DEAD.

"I FOLLOWED YOUR WISHES, AND PAID THEM A VISIT AT YOUR 'GRAVE-SITE...'"

"PARDON MY INTRUSION... BUT IT'S URGENT THAT I TALK WITH YOU."

WE WENT BACK TO YOUR MANSION, BUT BEFORE WE COULD GET DOWN TO TERMS, THERE WAS A MAJOR INTERRUPTION CALLED... JUGGERNAUT!

"HE LOOKED LIKE HALF-A-TON OF PURE RAGE. I THOUGHT IT WAS ALL OVER, BUT SOME HOW YOUR KIDS' DEALT WITH HIM."

"ONCE THAT WAS OVER, I GAVE THEM MY SONG AND DANCE, ORDERING THEM TO SPLIT UP INTO SMALLER UNITS AND SPREAD OUT ACROSS THE COUNTRY.

"AS THEY STOOD THERE, IN THEIR NEW OUTFITS, I TRIED NOT TO LOOK MS. GREY IN THE EYE. I KNEW THAT SHE WAS KEEPING YOUR SECRET--

"--AND HAD SUSPECTED THE REAL REASON FOR MY ORDER,...

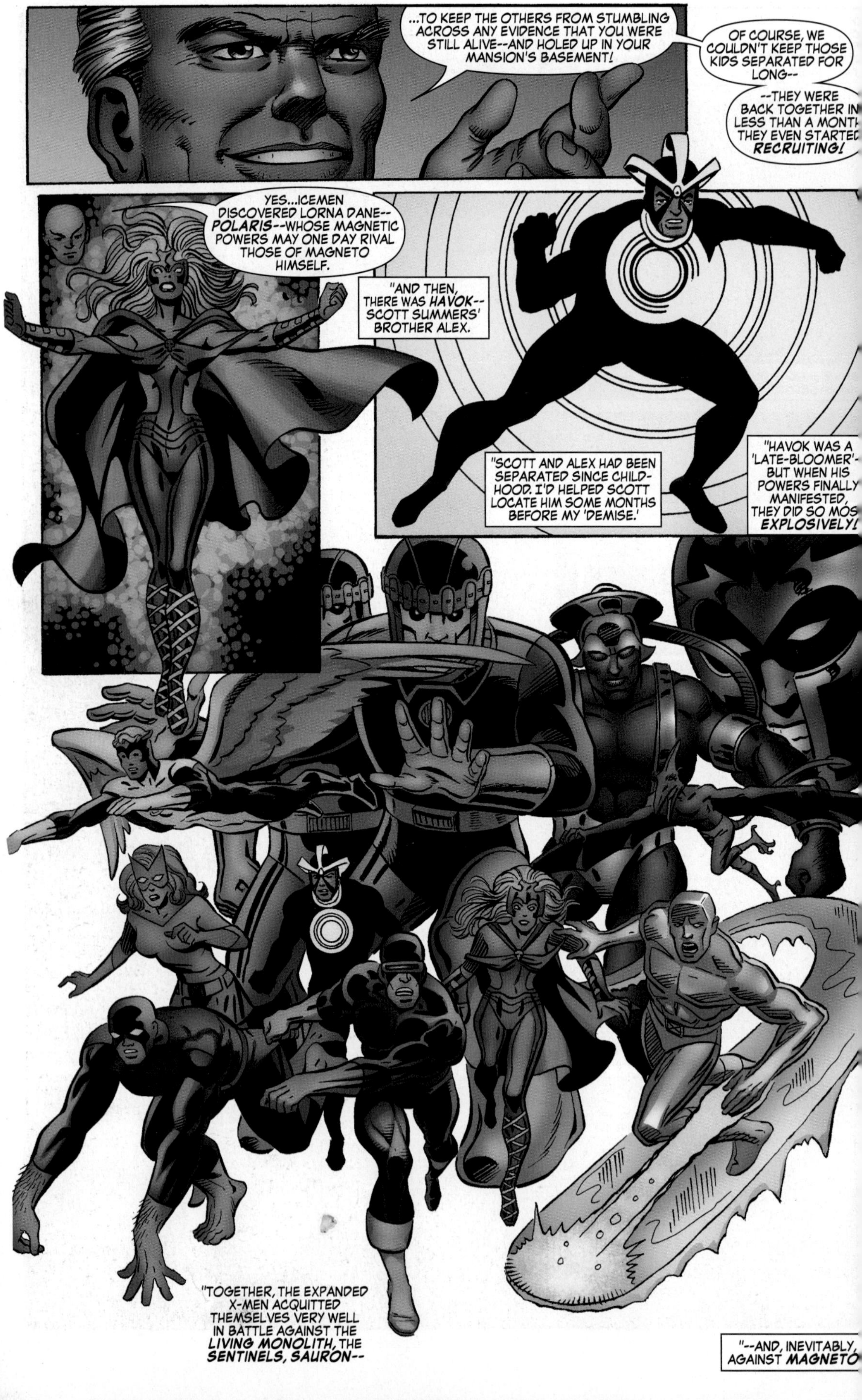
...TO KEEP THE OTHERS FROM STUMBLING ACROSS ANY EVIDENCE THAT YOU WERE STILL ALIVE--AND HOLED UP IN YOUR MANSION'S BASEMENT!
OF COURSE, WE COULDN'T KEEP THOSE KIDS SEPARATED FOR LONG--
--THEY WERE BACK TOGETHER IN LESS THAN A MONTH THEY EVEN STARTED RECRUITING!
YES...ICEMEN DISCOVERED LORNA DANE--POLARIS--WHOSE MAGNETIC POWERS MAY ONE DAY RIVAL THOSE OF MAGNETO HIMSELF.
"AND THEN, THERE WAS HAVOK--SCOTT SUMMERS' BROTHER ALEX.
"SCOTT AND ALEX HAD BEEN SEPARATED SINCE CHILD-HOOD. I'D HELPED SCOTT LOCATE HIM SOME MONTHS BEFORE MY 'DEMISE.'
"HAVOK WAS A 'LATE-BLOOMER'-BUT WHEN HIS POWERS FINALLY MANIFESTED, THEY DID SO MOS EXPLOSIVELY!
"TOGETHER, THE EXPANDED X-MEN ACQUITTED THEMSELVES VERY WELL IN BATTLE AGAINST THE LIVING MONOLITH, THE SENTINELS, SAURON--
"--AND, INEVITABLY, AGAINST MAGNETO

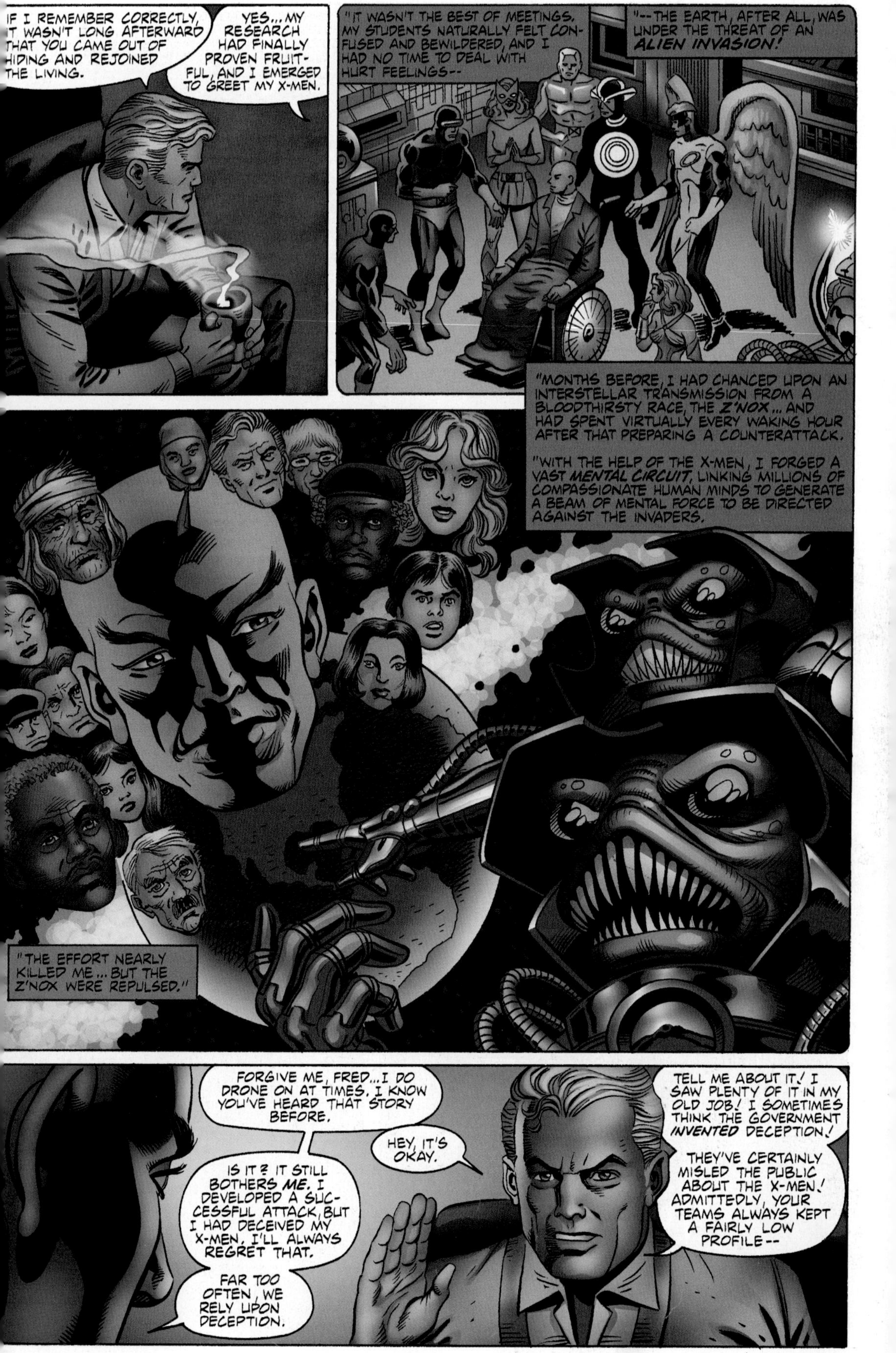

IF I REMEMBER CORRECTLY, IT WASN'T LONG AFTERWARD THAT YOU CAME OUT OF HIDING AND REJOINED THE LIVING.
YES... MY RESEARCH HAD FINALLY PROVEN FRUITFUL, AND I EMERGED TO GREET MY X-MEN.
"IT WASN'T THE BEST OF MEETINGS. MY STUDENTS NATURALLY FELT CONFUSED AND BEWILDERED, AND I HAD NO TIME TO DEAL WITH HURT FEELINGS--
"--THE EARTH, AFTER ALL, WAS UNDER THE THREAT OF AN ALIEN INVASION!
"MONTHS BEFORE, I HAD CHANCED UPON AN INTERSTELLAR TRANSMISSION FROM A BLOODTHIRSTY RACE, THE Z'NOX... AND HAD SPENT VIRTUALLY EVERY WAKING HOUR AFTER THAT PREPARING A COUNTERATTACK.
"WITH THE HELP OF THE X-MEN, I FORGED A VAST MENTAL CIRCUIT, LINKING MILLIONS OF COMPASSIONATE HUMAN MINDS TO GENERATE A BEAM OF MENTAL FORCE TO BE DIRECTED AGAINST THE INVADERS.
"THE EFFORT NEARLY KILLED ME... BUT THE Z'NOX WERE REPULSED."
FORGIVE ME, FRED... I DO DRONE ON AT TIMES. I KNOW YOU'VE HEARD THAT STORY BEFORE.
HEY, IT'S OKAY.
IS IT? IT STILL BOTHERS ME. I DEVELOPED A SUCCESSFUL ATTACK, BUT I HAD DECEIVED MY X-MEN. I'LL ALWAYS REGRET THAT.
FAR TOO OFTEN, WE RELY UPON DECEPTION.
TELL ME ABOUT IT! I SAW PLENTY OF IT IN MY OLD JOB! I SOMETIMES THINK THE GOVERNMENT INVENTED DECEPTION!
THEY'VE CERTAINLY MISLED THE PUBLIC ABOUT THE X-MEN! ADMITTEDLY, YOUR TEAMS ALWAYS KEPT A FAIRLY LOW PROFILE--

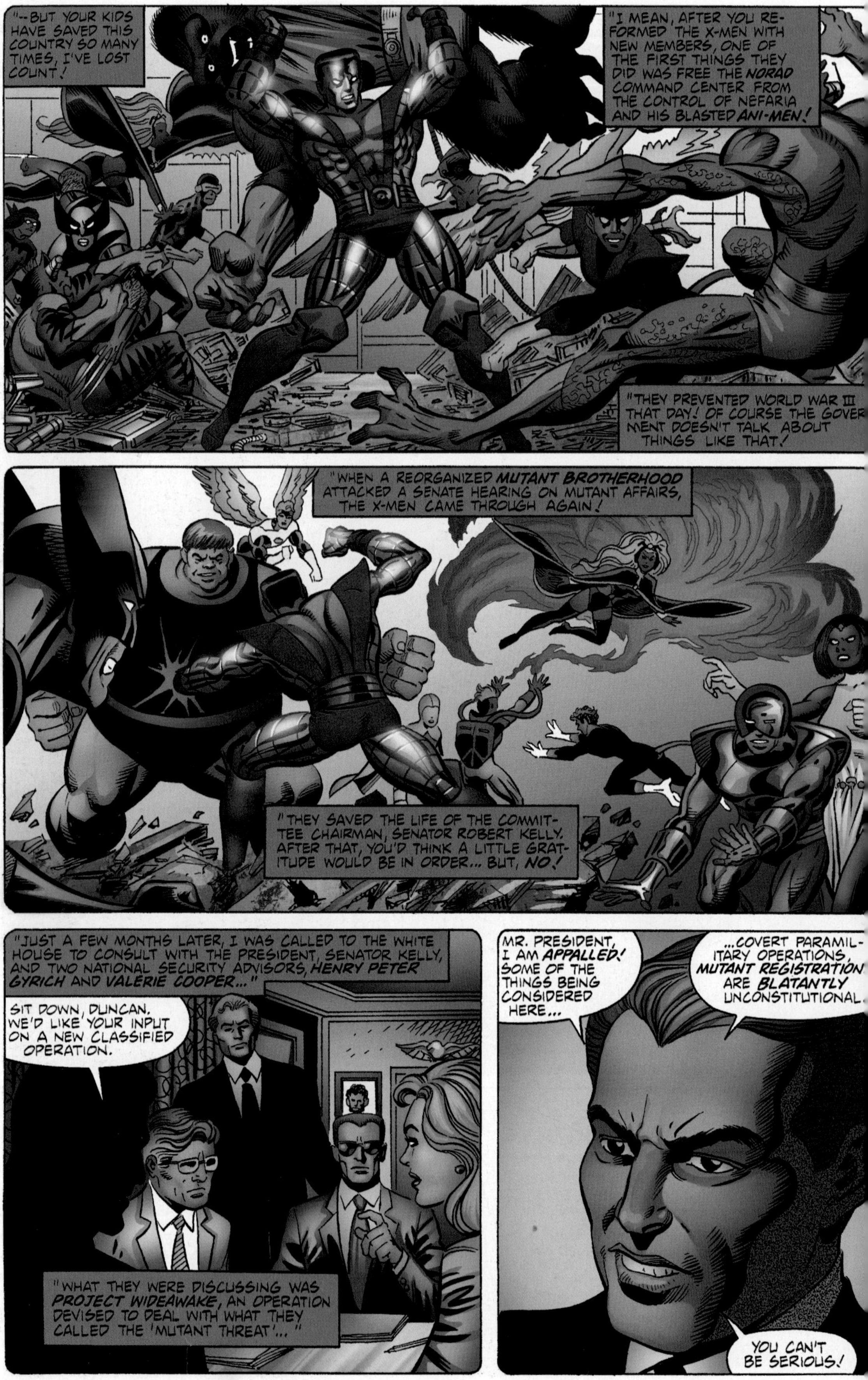
"--BUT YOUR KIDS HAVE SAVED THIS COUNTRY SO MANY TIMES, I'VE LOST COUNT!
"I MEAN, AFTER YOU RE-FORMED THE X-MEN WITH NEW MEMBERS, ONE OF THE FIRST THINGS THEY DID WAS FREE THE NORAD COMMAND CENTER FROM THE CONTROL OF NEFARIA AND HIS BLASTED ANI-MEN!
"THEY PREVENTED WORLD WAR III THAT DAY! OF COURSE THE GOVERNMENT DOESN'T TALK ABOUT THINGS LIKE THAT!
"WHEN A REORGANIZED MUTANT BROTHERHOOD ATTACKED A SENATE HEARING ON MUTANT AFFAIRS, THE X-MEN CAME THROUGH AGAIN!
"THEY SAVED THE LIFE OF THE COMMITTEE CHAIRMAN, SENATOR ROBERT KELLY. AFTER THAT, YOU'D THINK A LITTLE GRATITUDE WOULD BE IN ORDER... BUT, NO!
"JUST A FEW MONTHS LATER, I WAS CALLED TO THE WHITE HOUSE TO CONSULT WITH THE PRESIDENT, SENATOR KELLY, AND TWO NATIONAL SECURITY ADVISORS, HENRY PETER GYRICH AND VALERIE COOPER..."
SIT DOWN, DUNCAN. WE'D LIKE YOUR INPUT ON A NEW CLASSIFIED OPERATION.
"WHAT THEY WERE DISCUSSING WAS PROJECT WIDEAWAKE, AN OPERATION DEVISED TO DEAL WITH WHAT THEY CALLED THE 'MUTANT THREAT'..."
MR. PRESIDENT, I AM APPALLED! SOME OF THE THINGS BEING CONSIDERED HERE...
...COVERT PARAMILITARY OPERATIONS, MUTANT REGISTRATION ARE BLATANTLY UNCONSTITUTIONAL.
YOU CAN'T BE SERIOUS!

WELL, NOW HOLD ON THERE, FRED... WE'RE NOT ABOUT TO GO VIOLATING THE RIGHTS OF ANY GOOD CITIZEN!

WE'RE JUST TRYING TO MAKE CONTINGENCIES FOR DEALING WITH THREATS TO NATIONAL SECURITY. AMERICA HARDLY HAS A MONOPOLY ON MUTANTS, NOW DO WE?

NO, SIR, BUT--!

"I PUT UP THE BEST ARGUMENT I COULD..."

"...BUT INEVITABLY, I WAS DISMISSED. I GOT THE PICTURE THAT, WHATEVER PLANS THE ADMINISTRATION HAD IN REGARD TO MUTANTS--"

"--I WAS GOING TO BE OUT OF THE LOOP. GYRICH AND COOPER CLEARLY HAD THE PRESIDENT'S EAR..."

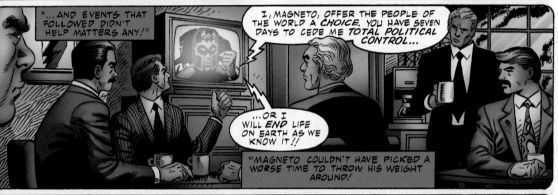

"...AND EVENTS THAT FOLLOWED DIDN'T HELP MATTERS ANY!"

I, MAGNETO, OFFER THE PEOPLE OF THE WORLD A *CHOICE*. YOU HAVE SEVEN DAYS TO CEDE ME *TOTAL POLITICAL CONTROL*...

...OR I WILL *END* LIFE ON EARTH AS WE KNOW IT!!

"MAGNETO COULDN'T HAVE PICKED A WORSE TIME TO THROW HIS WEIGHT AROUND!"

"I HEARD FROM YOU LATER HOW THE X-MEN WRECKED THAT LITTLE PLAN OF HIS. AND THEN, I DIDN'T HEAR ANY MORE UNTIL, ONE DAY..."

WHAT IN BLAZES IS GOING ON, DUNCAN?!

~?!?~

SPECIAL AGENT FRED DUNCAN

NICE TO SEE YOU TOO, GYRICH! TO WHAT DO I OWE THE PLEASURE?

ARE YOU TELLING ME THAT YOU *DON'T* KNOW?!

KNOW *WHAT*?

TRY ACCESSING YOUR FILES ON THE X-MEN... JUST *TRY!*

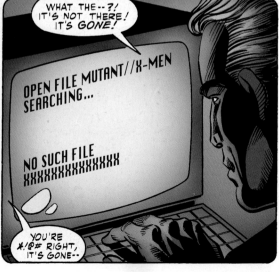

WHAT THE--?! IT'S NOT THERE! IT'S *GONE!*

OPEN FILE MUTANT//X-MEN
SEARCHING...

NO SUCH FILE
XXXXXXXXXXXXXX

YOU'RE *!@# RIGHT, IT'S GONE--

--IT'S BEEN *ERASED* FROM THE WHOLE ✱@#! FEDERAL DATA BANK! THERE'S NOT A SINGLE MEMORY-BYTE THAT SO MUCH AS *MENTIONS* THE X-MEN!

REALLY?

SONUVAGUN. SYSTEM MUST HAVE BEEN INFECTED BY SOME SORT OF OPEN-ENDED VIRUS... OR MAYBE A WORM.

IT'S THOSE ✱@!✱ *MUTIES!* THEY'VE DONE THIS SOME-HOW! BUT IT WON'T DO THEM ANY *GOOD!*

I WANT YOU TO START A NEW DATA-BASE IMMEDIATELY. PUT EVERYTHING YOU HAVE ON THE X-MEN INTO IT!

GEE, PETE, I DON'T THINK THAT'S *POSSIBLE!*

NOT POSSIBLE?

ALL PAPER FILES WERE ENTERED INTO THE OLD DATA BASE YEARS AGO. AFTER THAT, THEY WERE *SHREDDED...* NOT ENOUGH STORAGE SPACE. AND YOU WOULDN'T WANT TO RELY ON *MY* MEMORY! HECK, I CAN'T EVEN REMEMBER MY OWN SISTER'S BIRTHDAY!

DON'T GIVE ME THAT, DUNCAN! YOU MUST HAVE *SOMETHING!*

YOU'RE IN *CAHOOTS* WITH THEM, AREN'T YOU?! YOU ✱/@✱, I'LL HAVE YOUR JOB FOR THIS!

I DON'T REPORT TO YOU, GYRICH. I WORK FOR THE BUREAU!

NOT ANY MORE! ANYONE DEALING WITH MUTANT AF-FAIRS ANSWERS TO PROJECT WIDEAWAKE NOW-- AND THAT MEANS *ME!*

GOOD! THAT MAKES THIS MUCH SIMPLER! *HERE!*

WHAT'S THIS?

MY *RESIGNATION.* HOPE YOU LIKE IT, I'VE BEEN WORKING ON IT FOR WEEKS!

DON'T THINK IT HASN'T BEEN FUN.

"YOU REALLY SHOULD HAVE BEEN THERE...

...GYRICH WAS FIT TO BE TIED! I ONLY WISH I HAD SOME ROPE!

YOU TOOK A CHANCE IN QUITTING LIKE THAT, FRED. GYRICH MIGHT HAVE CAUSED YOU TROUBLE.

OH, HE *TRIED*... BUT I'D PLANNED FOR IT. AND I STILL HAVE A FEW FRIENDS AT THE CAPITOL.

EVEN SO, YOU SACRIFICED YOUR *CAREER* FOR US.

MY CAREER WAS OVER ANYWAY, CHARLES. WHAT I THOUGHT DIDN'T MATTER ANY MORE... THEY DIDN'T WANT TO HEAR IT.

WHAT AM I SAYING? YOU OF ALL PEOPLE *MUST* KNOW WHAT IT'S LIKE!

YES... I DO. MY POWERS... MY NATURE... HAVE KEPT ME AN OUTSIDER, AT ODDS WITH THE WORLD, MOST OF MY LIFE. EVEN IN LOVE, I'VE...

NO, IT DIDN'T MATTER HOW WELL I DID MY JOB, OR HOW MANY YEARS OF FAITHFUL SERVICE I'D PUT IN. THINGS HAD CHANGED AT THE TOP, AND I WAS SUDDENLY THE ODD MAN OUT. YOU DON'T KNOW--!

...WELL, A MAN CAN FIND HIMSELF IN A LOT OF ODD SITUATIONS, WHEN HE'S IN LOVE. HAVE I EVER TOLD YOU ABOUT THE *PRINCESS LILANDRA?*

PRINCESS--? NO...

YOU MAY FIND THIS HARD TO BELIEVE, FRED, BUT WHEN I'D TURNED MY PSIONIC BEAM SPACEWARD AGAINST THE Z'NOX, IT WAS SOMEHOW DETECTED, FAR ACROSS SPACE--

"--BY LILANDRA NERAMANI, PRINCESS-MAJESTRIX OF THE SHI'AR. CIVIL WAR HAD GRIPPED HER EMPIRE, AND LILANDRA FOLLOWED THE PATH OF MY BEAM...

"...TO EARTH, SEARCHING FOR SUPER-POWERED AID. MY X-MEN HELPED HER STOP THAT WAR...

"...AND WE FELL IN LOVE."

"I KNOW IT SOUNDS LIKE SOME MAD FANTASY, BUT IT'S *TRUE*... IT HAPPENED. DESPITE OUR DIFFERENCES IN ORIGIN-- IN *SPECIES!*--

"--I LOVED LILANDRA, AND SHE LOVED ME."

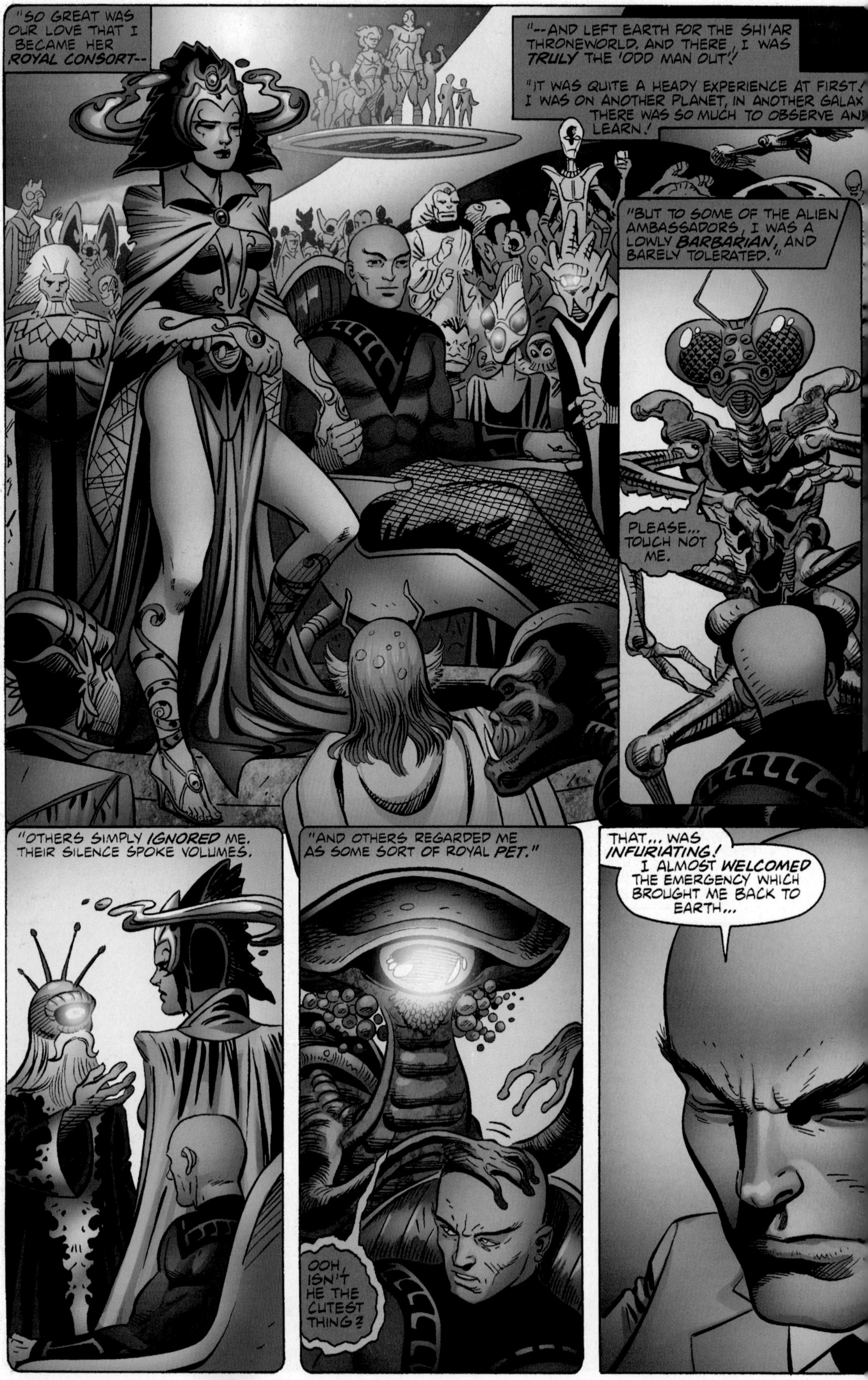

"SO GREAT WAS OUR LOVE THAT I BECAME HER ROYAL CONSORT--
"--AND LEFT EARTH FOR THE SHI'AR THRONEWORLD. AND THERE, I WAS TRULY THE 'ODD MAN OUT'!
"IT WAS QUITE A HEADY EXPERIENCE AT FIRST! I WAS ON ANOTHER PLANET, IN ANOTHER GALAX THERE WAS SO MUCH TO OBSERVE AN LEARN!
"BUT TO SOME OF THE ALIEN AMBASSADORS, I WAS A LOWLY BARBARIAN, AND BARELY TOLERATED."
PLEASE... TOUCH NOT ME.
"OTHERS SIMPLY IGNORED ME. THEIR SILENCE SPOKE VOLUMES.
"AND OTHERS REGARDED ME AS SOME SORT OF ROYAL PET."
OOH, ISN'T HE THE CUTEST THING?
THAT... WAS INFURIATING! I ALMOST WELCOMED THE EMERGENCY WHICH BROUGHT ME BACK TO EARTH...

"...THOUGH THE SITUATION AWAITING ME WAS A DESPERATE ONE, JEAN GREY'S PSI-POWERS WERE SEEMINGLY GROWING TO UNCONTROLLABLE LEVELS.

"AND THE THREAT OF DARK PHOENIX WAS ENDED ONLY THROUGH THE GREATEST OF SACRIFICES."

"THAT GROWTH CULMINATED IN THE EMERGANCE OF AN ENTITY WHICH CALLED ITSELF **DARK PHOENIX**!"

JEAN GREY

SINCE YOU BROUGHT THAT UP, CHARLES... I'D READ MS. GREY'S OBITUARY... WHO WAS THE MARVEL GIRL THAT JOINED THAT X-FACTOR BUNCH?

THE **REAL** JEAN GREY. THE PHOENIX, IT TURNS OUT--

--WAS A **COSMIC FORCE** WHICH HAD REPLICATED JEAN'S FORM AND CONSCIOUSNESS. THE YOUNG WOMAN WHO HAD BEEN MY STUDENT WAS STILL ALIVE...

...WONDERFULLY, MIRACULOUSLY-- **ALIVE**!

I CAUGHT **THAT**!

THE PROFESSOR'S POWERS MAY HAVE ALLOWED HIM TO ANALYZE AND CONFIRM MY "RESURRECTION"--

...I WAS JUST AS ASTOUNDED TO LEARN WHAT PHOENIX HAD DONE IN MY NAME.

I WISH YOU'D BEEN AROUND FOR MY **REVIVAL**, PROFESSOR.

--BUT HE'S STILL AS **AMAZED** BY IT AS EVERYONE. NOT THAT I BLAME HIM...

THINGS WOULD HAVE BEEN A LOT DIFFERENT FOR **X-FACTOR**...

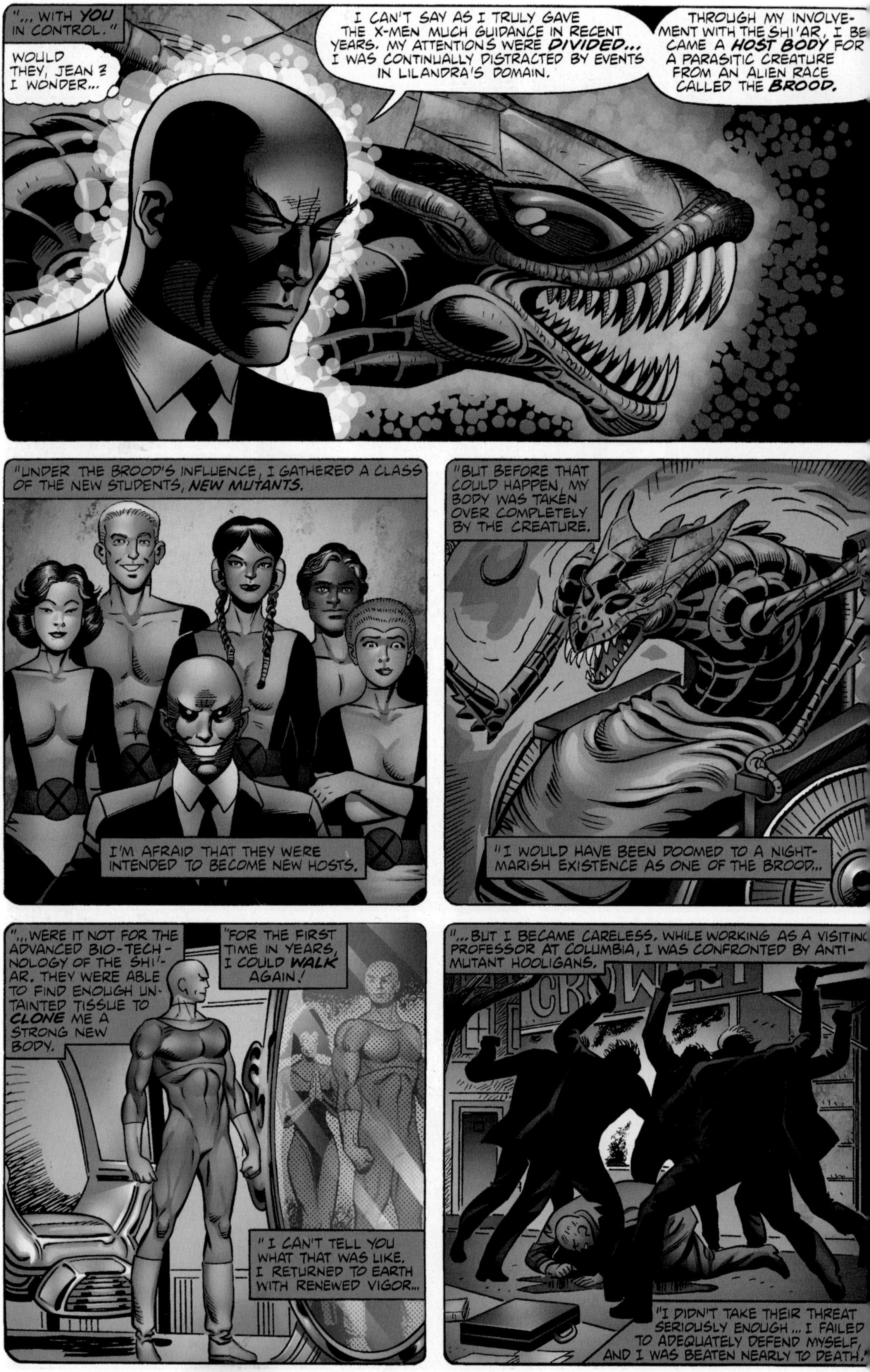
"... WITH YOU IN CONTROL."
WOULD THEY, JEAN? I WONDER...
I CAN'T SAY AS I TRULY GAVE THE X-MEN MUCH GUIDANCE IN RECENT YEARS. MY ATTENTIONS WERE DIVIDED... I WAS CONTINUALLY DISTRACTED BY EVENTS IN LILANDRA'S DOMAIN.
THROUGH MY INVOLVEMENT WITH THE SHI'AR, I BECAME A HOST BODY FOR A PARASITIC CREATURE FROM AN ALIEN RACE CALLED THE BROOD.
"UNDER THE BROOD'S INFLUENCE, I GATHERED A CLASS OF THE NEW STUDENTS, NEW MUTANTS.
I'M AFRAID THAT THEY WERE INTENDED TO BECOME NEW HOSTS.
"BUT BEFORE THAT COULD HAPPEN, MY BODY WAS TAKEN OVER COMPLETELY BY THE CREATURE.
"I WOULD HAVE BEEN DOOMED TO A NIGHTMARISH EXISTENCE AS ONE OF THE BROOD...
"...WERE IT NOT FOR THE ADVANCED BIO-TECHNOLOGY OF THE SHI'AR. THEY WERE ABLE TO FIND ENOUGH UNTAINTED TISSUE TO CLONE ME A STRONG NEW BODY.
"FOR THE FIRST TIME IN YEARS, I COULD WALK AGAIN!
"I CAN'T TELL YOU WHAT THAT WAS LIKE. I RETURNED TO EARTH WITH RENEWED VIGOR...
"...BUT I BECAME CARELESS. WHILE WORKING AS A VISITING PROFESSOR AT COLUMBIA, I WAS CONFRONTED BY ANTI-MUTANT HOOLIGANS.
"I DIDN'T TAKE THEIR THREAT SERIOUSLY ENOUGH... I FAILED TO ADEQUATELY DEFEND MYSELF, AND I WAS BEATEN NEARLY TO DEATH."

"MY WONDERFUL NEW BODY SOON BEGAN TO FAIL ME. DYING, I TURNED MY SCHOOL OVER TO MAGNETO.

"I WAS SAVED ONLY THROUGH THE INTERVENTION OF LILANDRA--

"-- WHO TRANSPORTED ME BACK TO THE SHI'AR GALAXY. THERE, I REGAINED MY VITALITY... BUT ONLY AFTER A LONG CONVELESCENCE."

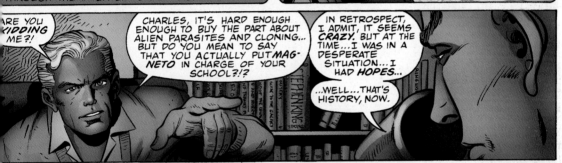

ARE YOU *KIDDING* ME?!

CHARLES, IT'S HARD ENOUGH ENOUGH TO BUY THE PART ABOUT ALIEN PARASITES AND CLONING... BUT DO YOU MEAN TO SAY THAT YOU ACTUALLY PUT *MAGNETO* IN CHARGE OF YOUR SCHOOL?!?

IN RETROSPECT, I ADMIT, IT SEEMS *CRAZY*. BUT AT THE TIME... I WAS IN A DESPERATE SITUATION... I HAD *HOPES*...

...WELL...THAT'S HISTORY, NOW.

"YOU MUST UNDERSTAND, I HAD NO FURTHER CONTACT WITH EARTH FOR MANY MONTHS. LILANDRA HAD BEEN DEPOSED, AND WE ROAMED HER GALAXY IN THE COMPANY OF SOME REBEL FREE-BOOTERS, THE *STARJAMMERS.*

"LIFE BECAME ONE VAST ADVENTURE.

"I BECAME LILANDRA'S *WARLORD*, FOMENTING A REBELLION TO RETURN HER TO POWER.

"WE HAD LITTLE TIME TO OURSELVES...

CHARLES...//

...YOU SEEM PENSIVE. IS THERE A PROBLEM WITH THE PLAN OF ATTACK?

EH? NO... NO, ALL SHOULD GO WELL.

"I REALIZED THAT HER FIRST DUTY WOULD ALWAYS BE TO HER EMPIRE. AGAIN, I WAS THE OUTSIDER.

"AT ANY RATE, ON OUR NEXT FORAY, THE STAR-JAMMERS AND I WERE CAPTURED BY A BAND OF WAR-SKRULLS, WHO EMPLOYED A BIZARRE BIO-TEMPLATE. IT NOT ONLY HELD US CAPTIVE--

"THROUGH THAT POWER, HE WAS ABLE TO CONTROL LILANDRA... AND THROUGH HER, THE NEWLY-WON THRONE OF THE SHI'AR EMPIRE!

"IRONIC, ISN'T IT? ANOTHER MASQUERADE, ANOTHER DECEPTION... ONLY THIS TIME, WE WERE ALL VICTIMS!

"--IT ENABLED THEM TO REPLICATE US RIGHT DOWN TO THE MOLECULAR LEVEL... MY SKRULL-DOUBLE EVEN POSSESSED MY MENTAL POWERS.

"IF THE X-MEN HADN'T BEEN DRAWN INTO THE CONFLICT, WHO KNOWS WHAT MIGHT HAVE COME TO PASS? BUT DRAWN IN THEY WERE...

"AND WITH THEIR SUPPORT, I WAS FINALLY ABLE TO OVERCOME MY SKRULL DOPPELGANGER.

"BUT I WAS NOT YET DONE WITH BATTLE.

"THROUGH MY X-MEN, I LEARNED OF A GREAT EVIL LOOSE ON EARTH... AN OLD, OLD ENEMY... THE SHADOW KING!

"WE RETURNED TO OPPOSE HIM. I PERSONALLY PUT AN END TO HIM...

...BUT IN DOING SO, I LOST THE USE OF MY LEGS ONCE MORE.

CHARLES, I... I'M SORRY.

LORD, BUT THAT SOUNDS INADEQUATE.

I'D READ WHERE YOU WERE WALKING AGAIN. WHEN I SAW YOU...BACK IN THAT WHEELCHAIR...I WANTED TO ASK, BUT I DIDN'T WANT TO OPEN ANY OLD WOUNDS.

DON'T LET IT BOTHER YOU, FRED...

...I'M TRYING NOT TO LET IT BOTHER ME. I'VE LIVED THROUGH THIS BEFORE.

AND I STILL HAVE MY LIFE, AFTER ALL ...AND MY WORK.

SPEAKING OF WORK, IT *IS* GOOD TO SEE YOU LOOKING SO PROSPEROUS. YOU'VE MADE QUITE A LIFE FOR YOURSELF.

YEAH, MY EXPERIENCE PAID OFF NICELY IN THE PRIVATE SECTOR. BEING A SECURITY CONSULTANT GOT ME A NICE HOME-- AND PLENTY OF FREE TIME FOR MY OTHER INTERESTS.

I'VE BEEN WRITING A *BOOK*...

...AND I HOPE TO BLOW THE LID OFF THE GOVERNMENT'S MIS-HANDLING OF ANTI-MUTANT HYSTERIA!

THANKS TO THE FREEDOM OF INFORMATION ACT, I'VE BEEN ABLE TO DIG UP PLENTY OF DIRT.

THEY'VE DENIED ME A LOT, CLAIMING "NATIONAL SECURITY," BUT I STILL HAVE ENOUGH TO MAKE THEM SWEAT.

FRED, ABOUT THIS BOOK--!

YOU NEEDN'T WORRY-- NOTHING IN THE BOOK WILL COMPROMISE YOU OR THE X-MEN! YOU HAVE MY WORD ON THAT!

I'M NOT WORRIED ABOUT *US*. THIS BOOK COULD PUT *YOU* IN CONSIDERABLE DANGER... THERE ARE MANY PEOPLE WHO WON'T LIKE ITS MESSAGE.

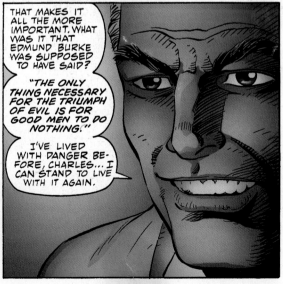

THAT MAKES IT ALL THE MORE IMPORTANT. WHAT WAS IT THAT EDMUND BURKE WAS SUPPOSED TO HAVE SAID?

"THE ONLY THING NECESSARY FOR THE TRIUMPH OF EVIL IS FOR GOOD MEN TO DO NOTHING."

I'VE LIVED WITH DANGER BE-FORE, CHARLES... I CAN STAND TO LIVE WITH IT AGAIN.

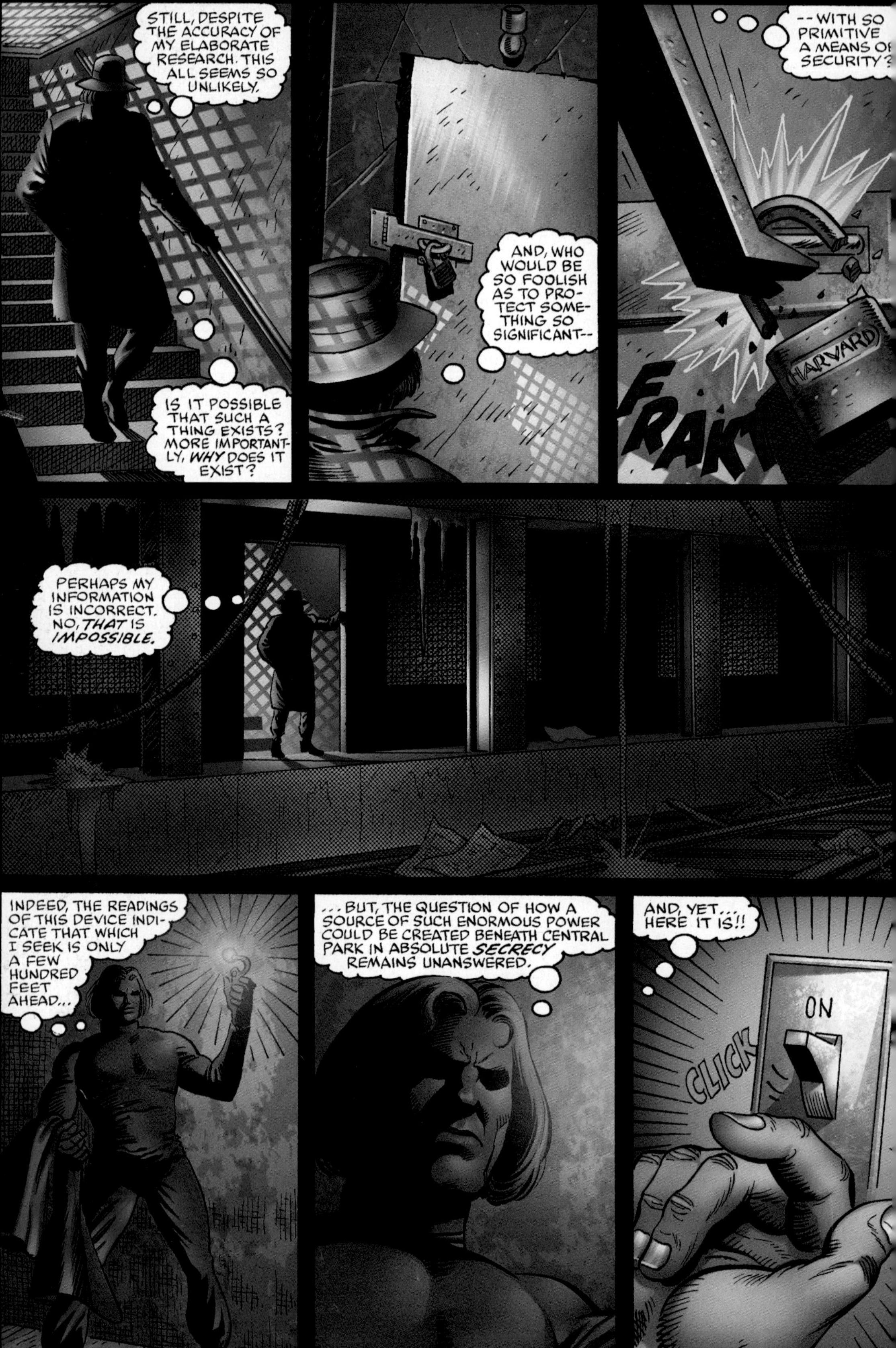
STILL, DESPITE THE ACCURACY OF MY ELABORATE RESEARCH. THIS ALL SEEMS SO UNLIKELY.
IS IT POSSIBLE THAT SUCH A THING EXISTS? MORE IMPORTANTLY, WHY DOES IT EXIST?
AND, WHO WOULD BE SO FOOLISH AS TO PROTECT SOMETHING SO SIGNIFICANT--
--WITH SO PRIMITIVE A MEANS OF SECURITY?
HARVARD
FRAK
PERHAPS MY INFORMATION IS INCORRECT. NO, THAT IS IMPOSSIBLE.
INDEED, THE READINGS OF THIS DEVICE INDICATE THAT WHICH I SEEK IS ONLY A FEW HUNDRED FEET AHEAD...
...BUT, THE QUESTION OF HOW A SOURCE OF SUCH ENORMOUS POWER COULD BE CREATED BENEATH CENTRAL PARK IN ABSOLUTE SECRECY REMAINS UNANSWERED.
AND, YET... HERE IT IS!!
ON
CLICK

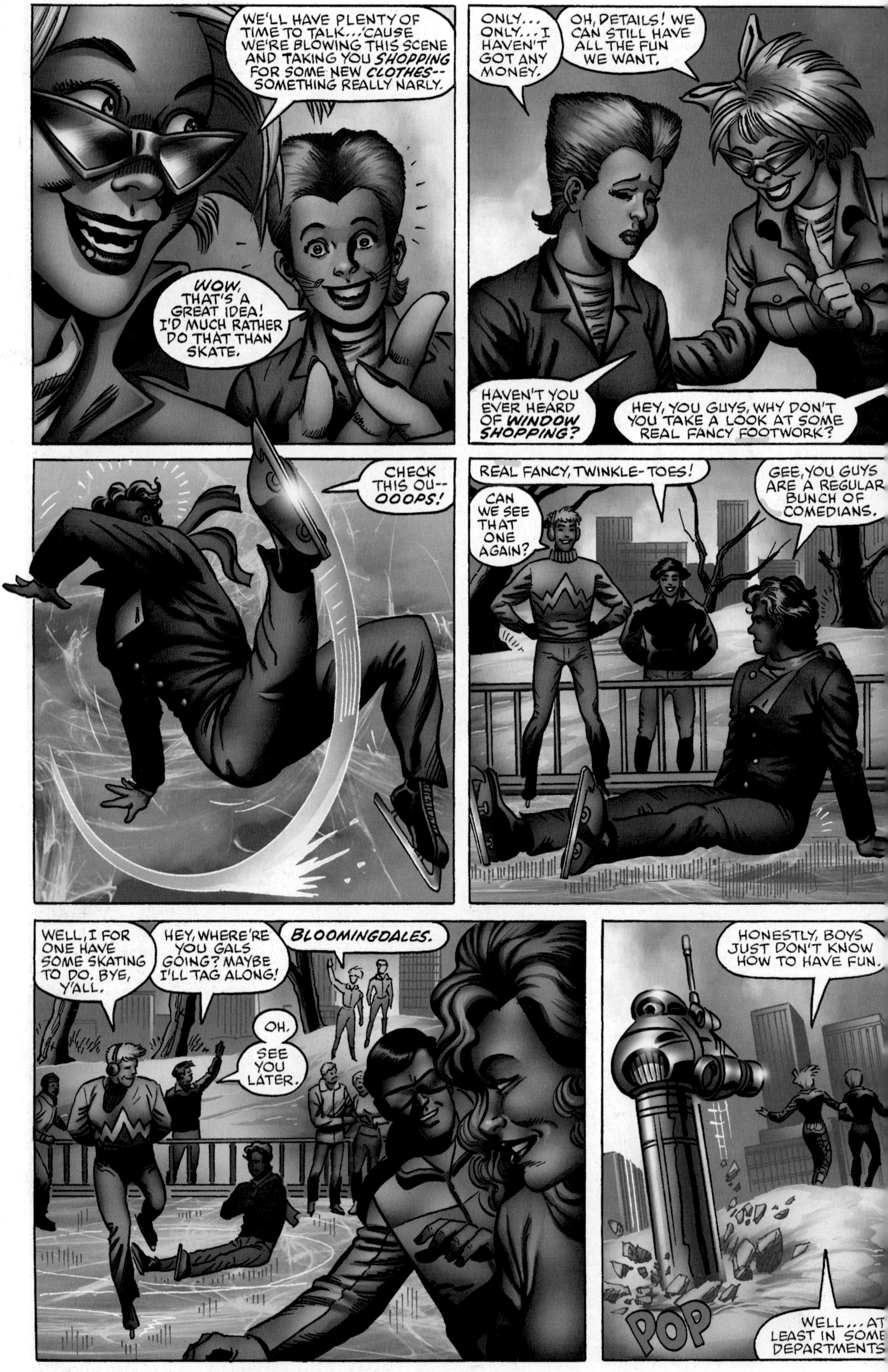
WE'LL HAVE PLENTY OF TIME TO TALK...'CAUSE WE'RE BLOWING THIS SCENE AND TAKING YOU SHOPPING FOR SOME NEW CLOTHES-- SOMETHING REALLY NARLY.
WOW, THAT'S A GREAT IDEA! I'D MUCH RATHER DO THAT THAN SKATE.
ONLY... ONLY... I HAVEN'T GOT ANY MONEY.
OH, DETAILS! WE CAN STILL HAVE ALL THE FUN WE WANT.
HAVEN'T YOU EVER HEARD OF WINDOW SHOPPING?
HEY, YOU GUYS, WHY DON'T YOU TAKE A LOOK AT SOME REAL FANCY FOOTWORK?
CHECK THIS OU-- OOOPS!
REAL FANCY, TWINKLE-TOES!
CAN WE SEE THAT ONE AGAIN?
GEE, YOU GUYS ARE A REGULAR BUNCH OF COMEDIANS.
WELL, I FOR ONE HAVE SOME SKATING TO DO. BYE, Y'ALL.
HEY, WHERE'RE YOU GALS GOING? MAYBE I'LL TAG ALONG!
BLOOMINGDALES.
OH. SEE YOU LATER.
HONESTLY, BOYS JUST DON'T KNOW HOW TO HAVE FUN.
POP
WELL... AT LEAST IN SOME DEPARTMENTS

HAVING DEDUCED ALL PROBABILITIES, THIS DUO APPEARED EXACTLY AS I ANTICIPATED. WHILE OTHERS MIGHT RELY UPON CHANCE, I RELY SOLELY UPON KNOWLEDGE AND PLANNING.

THE MOMENT HAS COME.

EVERYTHING IS IN READINESS. MY GREATEST CREATION AWAITS ONLY THE *SPARK OF LIFE*--

SURELY, THIS ANDROID WILL NOT BE FLAWED LIKE HIS PRIMITIVE PREDECESSOR, CONSTRUCTED UPON ERRONEOUS, SHALLOW RESEARCH GATHERED BY THE SIMPLE-MINDED *REED RICHARDS*.

-- SOMETHING I WILL NOW PROVIDE !

THE INFORMATION PROVIDED BY THESE AMAZINGLY ADVANCED CIRCUITS CAN BE SYNTHESIZED IN A MANNER FAR BEYOND THE COMPREHENSION OF THE SO-CALLED *MISTER FANTASTIC*.

FEEL THE *POWER* THAT SURGES THROUGH YOU--

CLICK

--AND RISE FROM YOUR LIFELESS STATE TO GREET THE FACE OF YOUR *MASTER!*

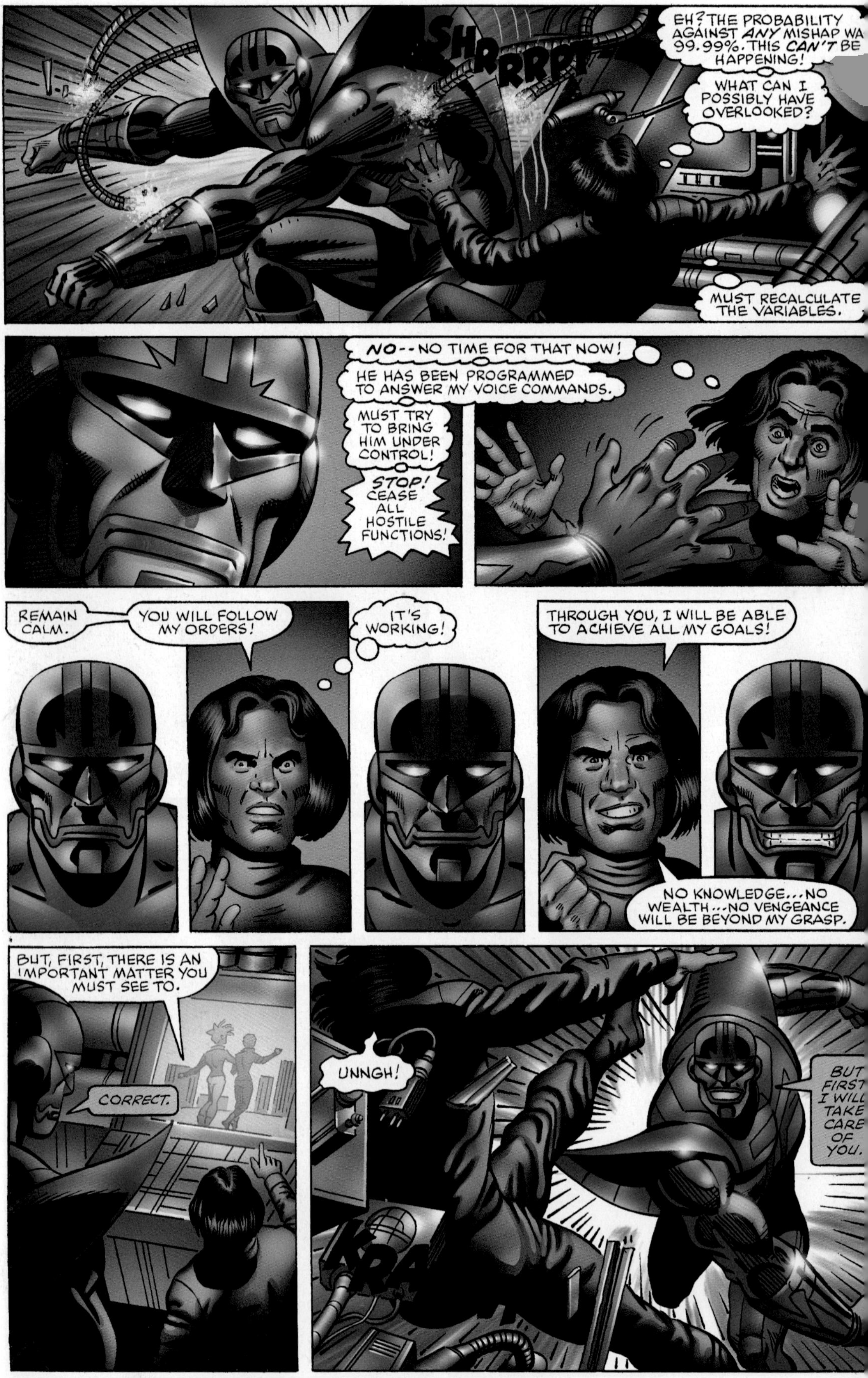

SHRRRPT
EH? THE PROBABILITY AGAINST ANY MISHAP WA 99.99%. THIS CAN'T BE HAPPENING!
WHAT CAN I POSSIBLY HAVE OVERLOOKED?
MUST RECALCULATE THE VARIABLES.
NO-- NO TIME FOR THAT NOW!
HE HAS BEEN PROGRAMMED TO ANSWER MY VOICE COMMANDS.
MUST TRY TO BRING HIM UNDER CONTROL!
STOP! CEASE ALL HOSTILE FUNCTIONS!
REMAIN CALM.
YOU WILL FOLLOW MY ORDERS!
IT'S WORKING!
THROUGH YOU, I WILL BE ABLE TO ACHIEVE ALL MY GOALS!
NO KNOWLEDGE... NO WEALTH... NO VENGEANCE WILL BE BEYOND MY GRASP.
BUT, FIRST, THERE IS AN IMPORTANT MATTER YOU MUST SEE TO.
CORRECT.
UNNGH!
BUT FIRST I WILL TAKE CARE OF YOU.

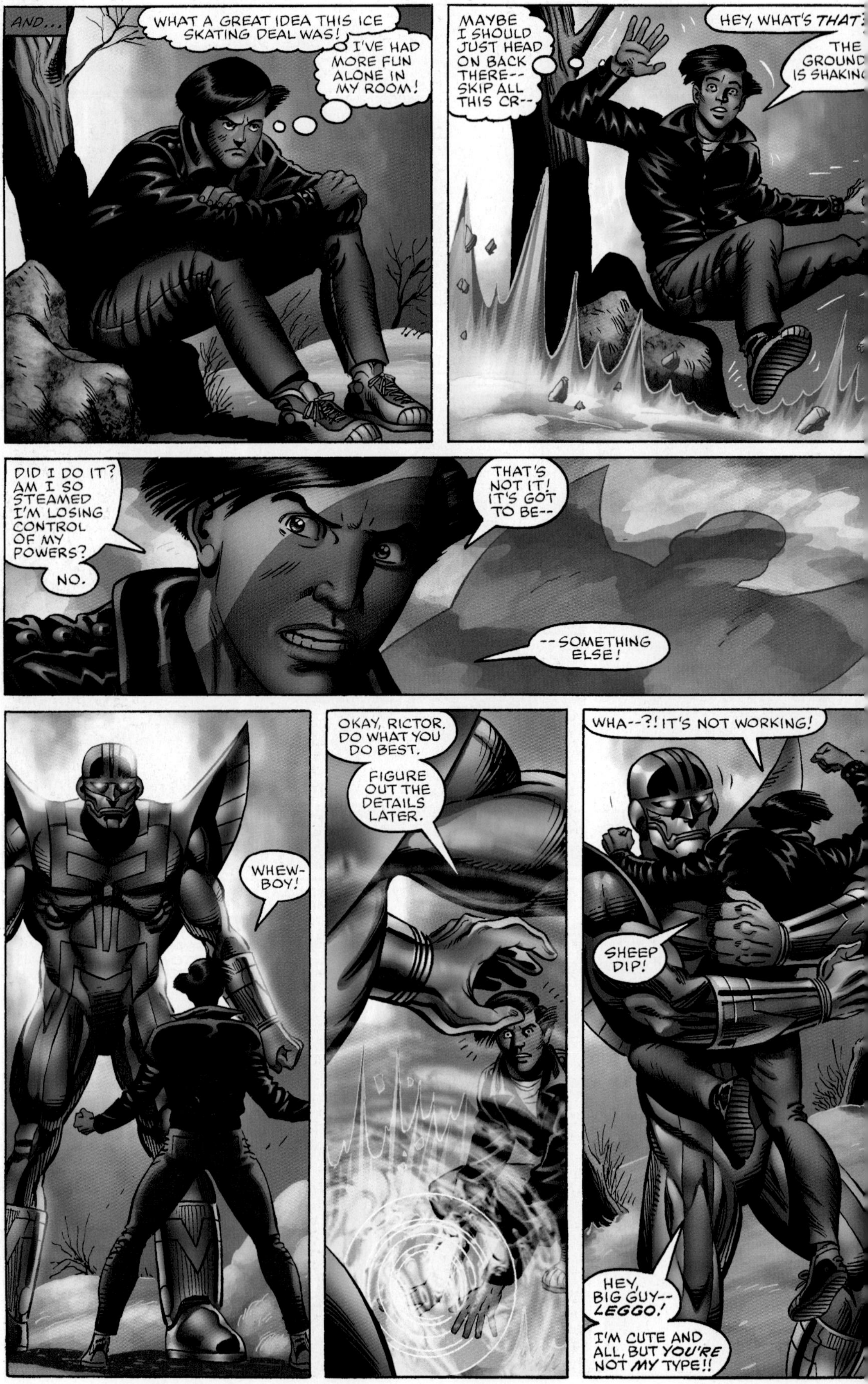
AND...
WHAT A GREAT IDEA THIS ICE SKATING DEAL WAS!
I'VE HAD MORE FUN ALONE IN MY ROOM!
MAYBE I SHOULD JUST HEAD ON BACK THERE-- SKIP ALL THIS CR--
HEY, WHAT'S *THAT*
THE GROUND IS SHAKIN
DID I DO IT? AM I SO STEAMED I'M LOSING CONTROL OF MY POWERS?
NO.
THAT'S NOT IT! IT'S GOT TO BE--
--SOMETHING ELSE!
WHEW-BOY!
OKAY, RICTOR. DO WHAT YOU DO BEST.
FIGURE OUT THE DETAILS LATER.
WHA--?! IT'S NOT WORKING!
SHEEP DIP!
HEY, BIG GUY-- *LEGGO!*
I'M CUTE AND ALL, BUT *YOU'RE* NOT *MY* TYPE!!

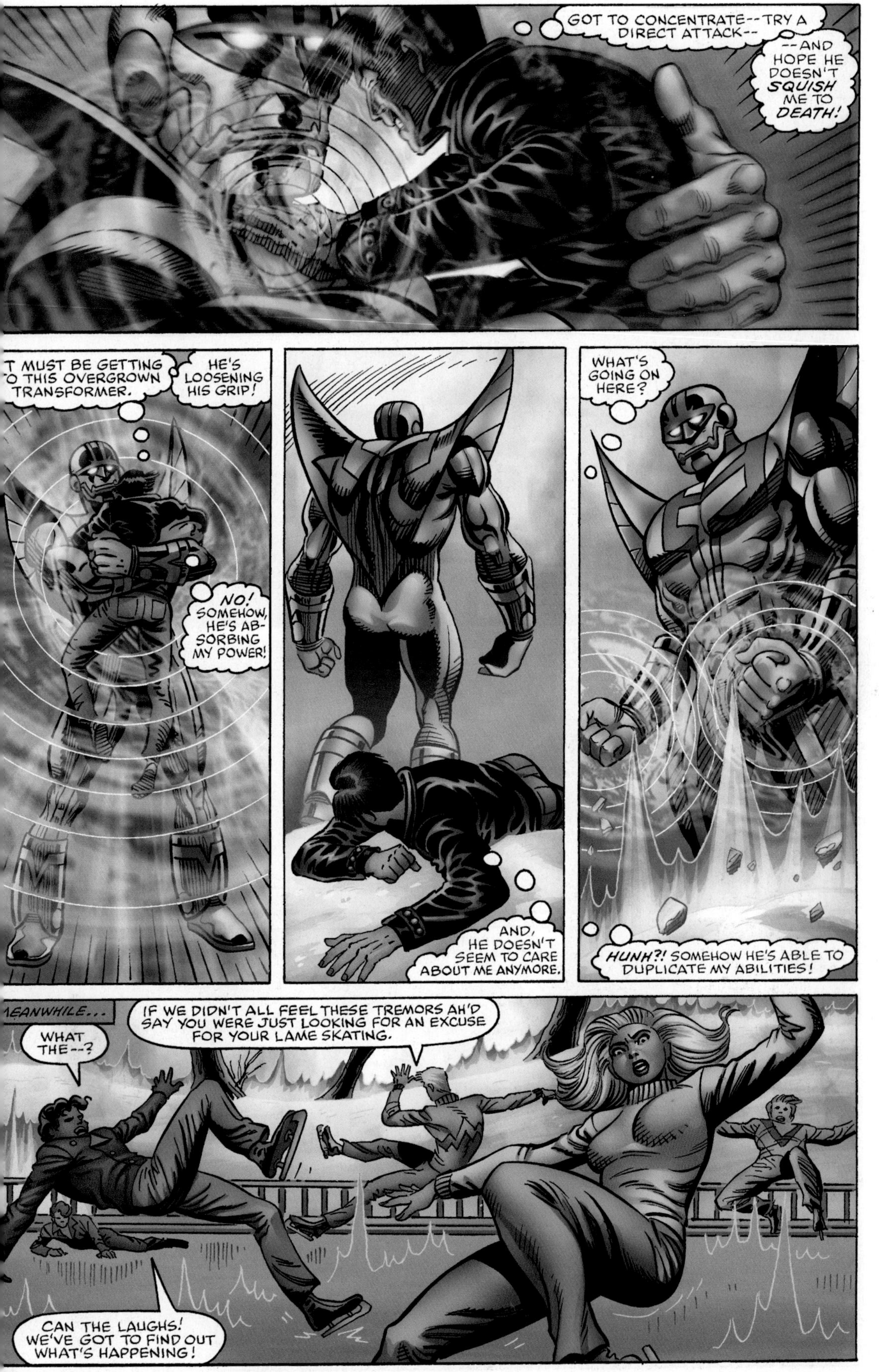

GOT TO CONCENTRATE-- TRY A DIRECT ATTACK--
--AND HOPE HE DOESN'T SQUISH ME TO DEATH!
T MUST BE GETTING TO THIS OVERGROWN TRANSFORMER.
HE'S LOOSENING HIS GRIP!
NO! SOMEHOW, HE'S ABSORBING MY POWER!
AND, HE DOESN'T SEEM TO CARE ABOUT ME ANYMORE.
WHAT'S GOING ON HERE?
HUNH?! SOMEHOW HE'S ABLE TO DUPLICATE MY ABILITIES!
MEANWHILE...
WHAT THE--?
IF WE DIDN'T ALL FEEL THESE TREMORS AH'D SAY YOU WERE JUST LOOKING FOR AN EXCUSE FOR YOUR LAME SKATING.
CAN THE LAUGHS! WE'VE GOT TO FIND OUT WHAT'S HAPPENING!

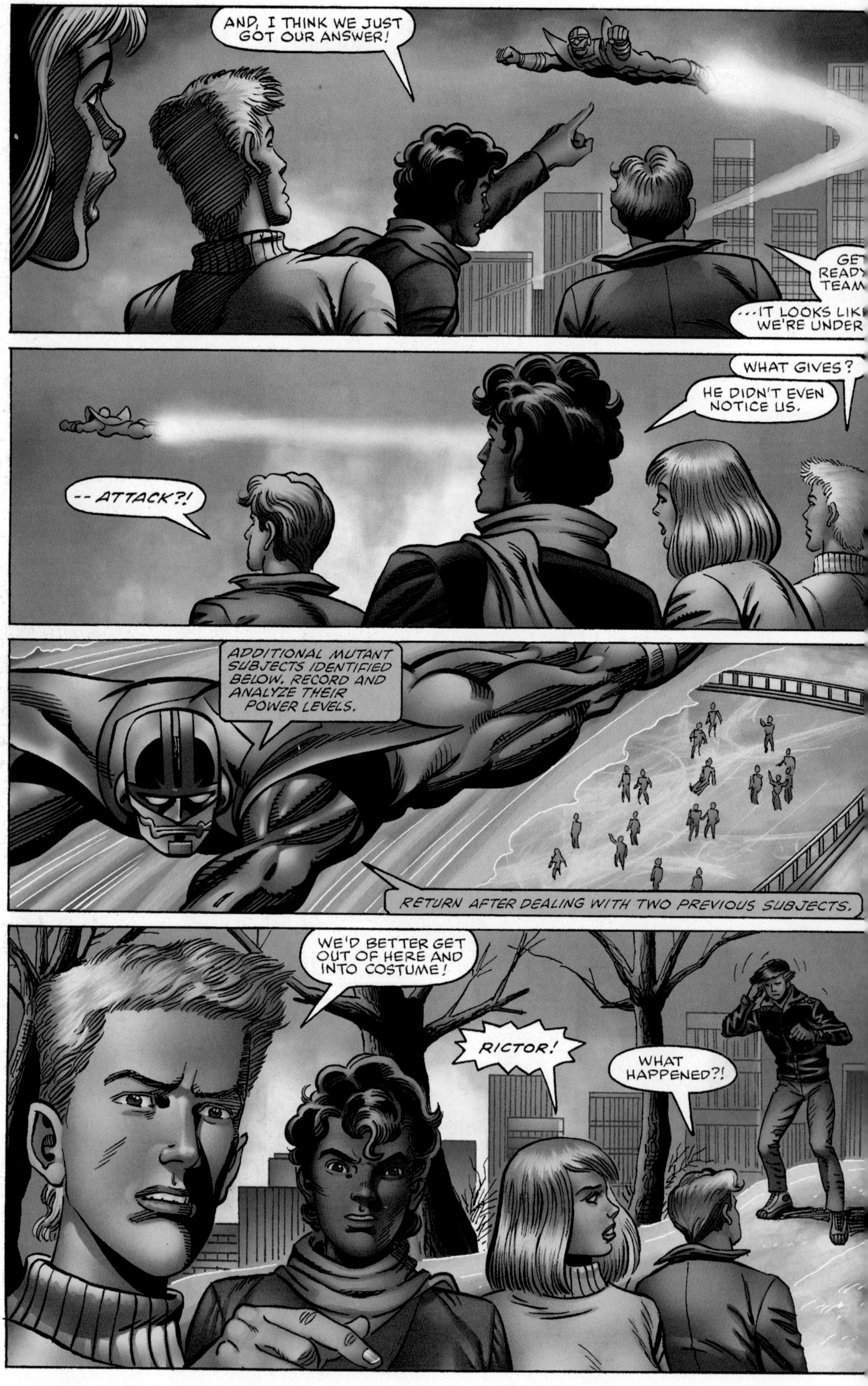

AND, I THINK WE JUST GOT OUR ANSWER!
GET READY TEAM
...IT LOOKS LIK WE'RE UNDER
--ATTACK?!
WHAT GIVES?
HE DIDN'T EVEN NOTICE US.
ADDITIONAL MUTANT SUBJECTS IDENTIFIED BELOW. RECORD AND ANALYZE THEIR POWER LEVELS.
RETURN AFTER DEALING WITH TWO PREVIOUS SUBJECTS.
WE'D BETTER GET OUT OF HERE AND INTO COSTUME!
RICTOR!
WHAT HAPPENED?!

HAND ME MINE-- *QUICK!*

ARE YOU SURE YOU'RE UP FOR THIS?

MAYBE YOU SHOULD JUST SIT THIS ONE OUT.

NO WAY!

WE'RE ALL PART OF THIS TEAM-- AND I'M THE ONLY ONE WHO HAS A SCORE TO SETTLE WITH...WELL, WHATEVER THAT THING IS!

THEN, *LET'S GO!*

OH, MY WORD!

WILL YOU LOOK AT THOSE RUFFIANS!

AND THEIR OUTFITS!

WHAT IS HAPPENING TO THIS CITY?

THERE, THERE, PRECIOUS!

BANK

AND...

WHAT DO YOU THINK?

I THINK YOU LOOK JUST *PEACHY!*

DON'T YOU THINK IT LOOKS JUST A LITTLE BIT...*SILLY?*

DON'T BE RIDICULOUS! YOU'VE NEVER LOOKED BETTER!

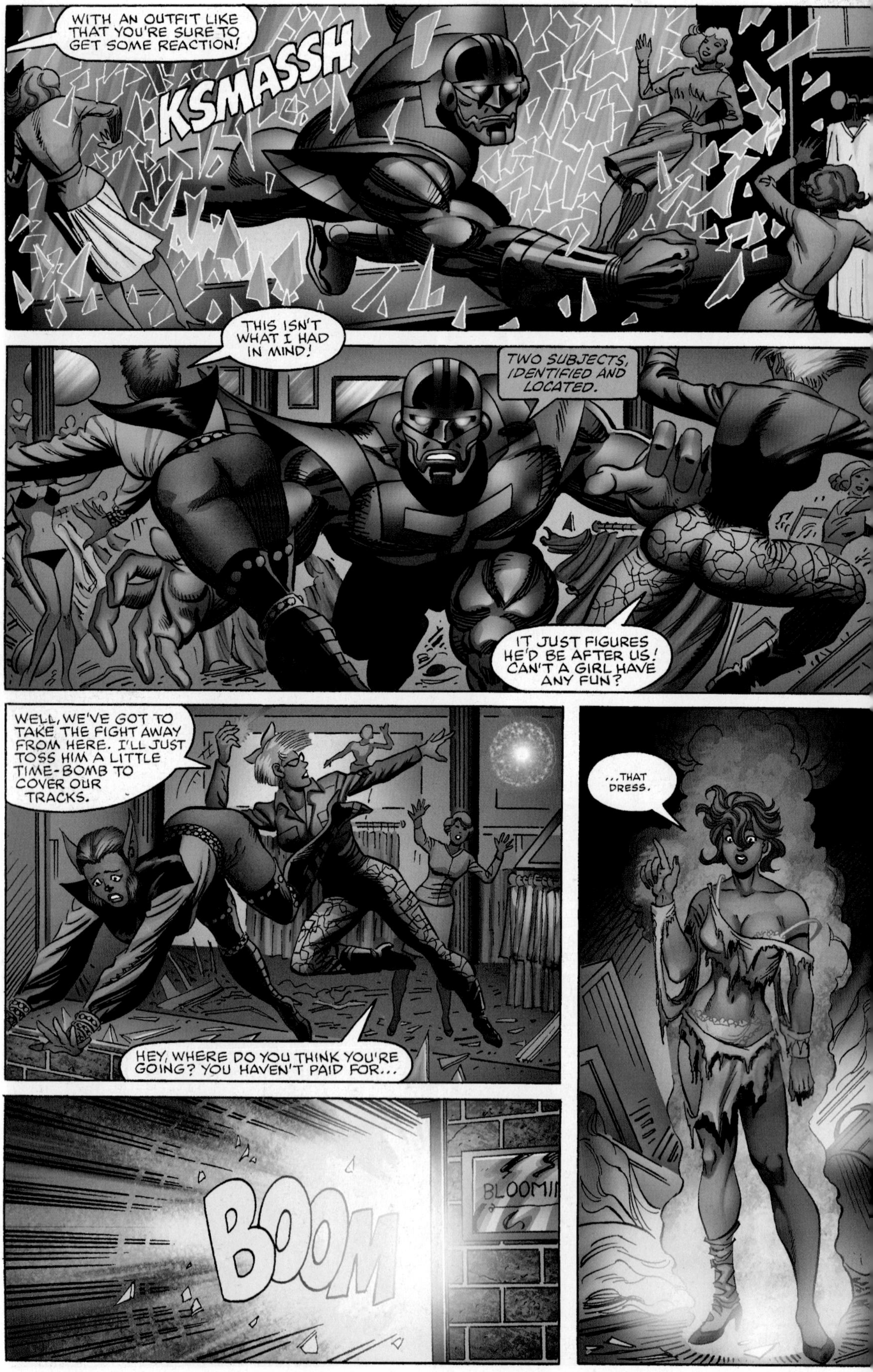
WITH AN OUTFIT LIKE THAT YOU'RE SURE TO GET SOME REACTION!
KSMASSH
THIS ISN'T WHAT I HAD IN MIND!
TWO SUBJECTS, IDENTIFIED AND LOCATED.
IT JUST FIGURES HE'D BE AFTER US! CAN'T A GIRL HAVE ANY FUN?
WELL, WE'VE GOT TO TAKE THE FIGHT AWAY FROM HERE. I'LL JUST TOSS HIM A LITTLE TIME-BOMB TO COVER OUR TRACKS.
HEY, WHERE DO YOU THINK YOU'RE GOING? YOU HAVEN'T PAID FOR...
...THAT DRESS.
BOOM
BLOOMI

WELL, IT LOOKS LIKE THE GANG'S ALL HERE.

YOU WON'T BELIEVE WHAT WE JUST SAW BACK THERE. SOME SORT OF HUGE ROBOT!

YEAH, WE KINDA HAD AN IDEA.

AND, HE'S AFTER US! WE'VE GOT TO DRAW HIM AWAY FROM THIS CROWDED AREA!

CENTRAL PARK'S THE ONLY OPEN SPACE!

THEN, THE PARK IT IS!

ISN'T THERE ANY WAY WE CAN ESCAPE THIS MADNESS?

WHAT'S NEXT?

OH, MY! THAT'S IT! WE'RE HEADING FOR THE HILLS!

PERHAPS IT WOULD BE WISE TO SEEK COVER, PRECIOUS.

COVER? I'M TALKING ABOUT BEVERLY HILLS!

WELL, WELL. LOOKS LIKE MR. MACHINE HAS DECIDED TO JOIN US.

NOW, SEE HERE, BUB. WE HAD A BUSY DAY PLANNED AND YOU'RE MESSING EVERYTHING UP!

THAT MAKES ME MAD!

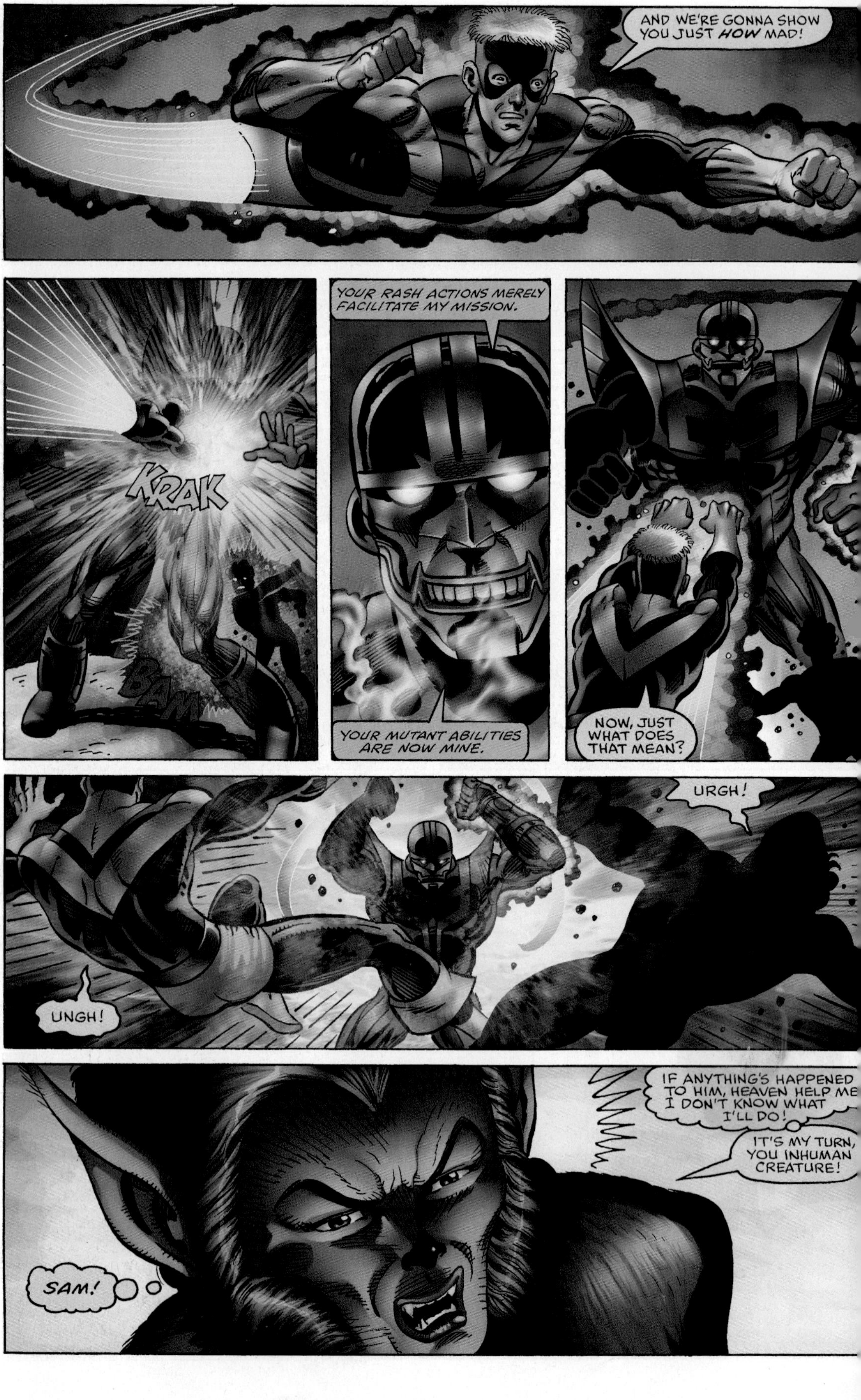
AND WE'RE GONNA SHOW YOU JUST *HOW* MAD!
KRAK
BAM
YOUR RASH ACTIONS MERELY FACILITATE MY MISSION.
YOUR MUTANT ABILITIES ARE NOW MINE.
NOW, JUST WHAT DOES THAT MEAN?
URGH!
UNGH!
IF ANYTHING'S HAPPENED TO HIM, HEAVEN HELP ME I DON'T KNOW WHAT I'LL DO!
IT'S MY TURN, YOU INHUMAN CREATURE!
SAM!

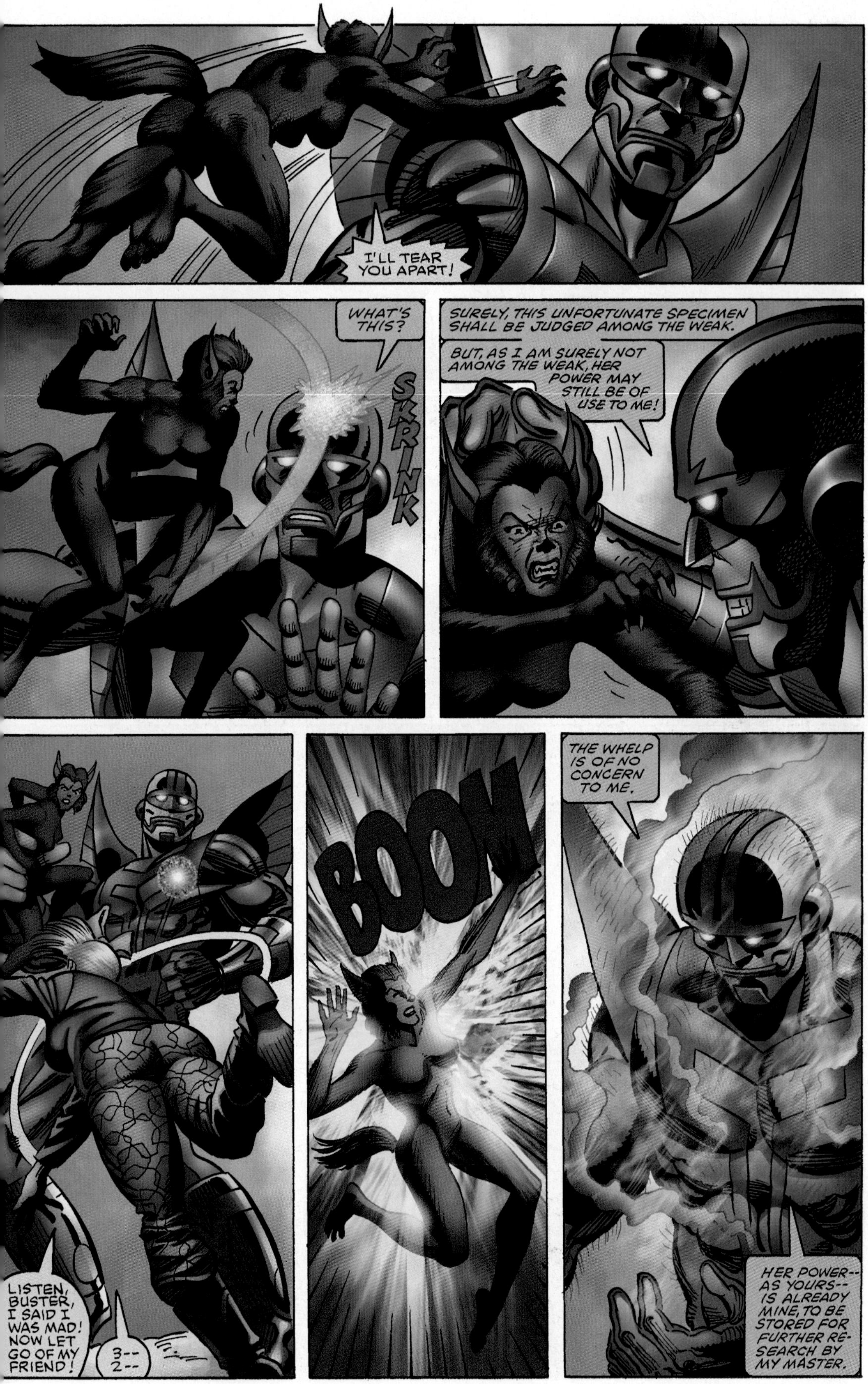
I'LL TEAR YOU APART!
WHAT'S THIS?
SKRINK
SURELY, THIS UNFORTUNATE SPECIMEN SHALL BE JUDGED AMONG THE WEAK.
BUT, AS I AM SURELY NOT AMONG THE WEAK, HER POWER MAY STILL BE OF USE TO ME!
LISTEN, BUSTER, I SAID I WAS MAD! NOW LET GO OF MY FRIEND!
3-- 2--
BOOM
THE WHELP IS OF NO CONCERN TO ME.
HER POWER-- AS YOURS-- IS ALREADY MINE, TO BE STORED FOR FURTHER RESEARCH BY MY MASTER.

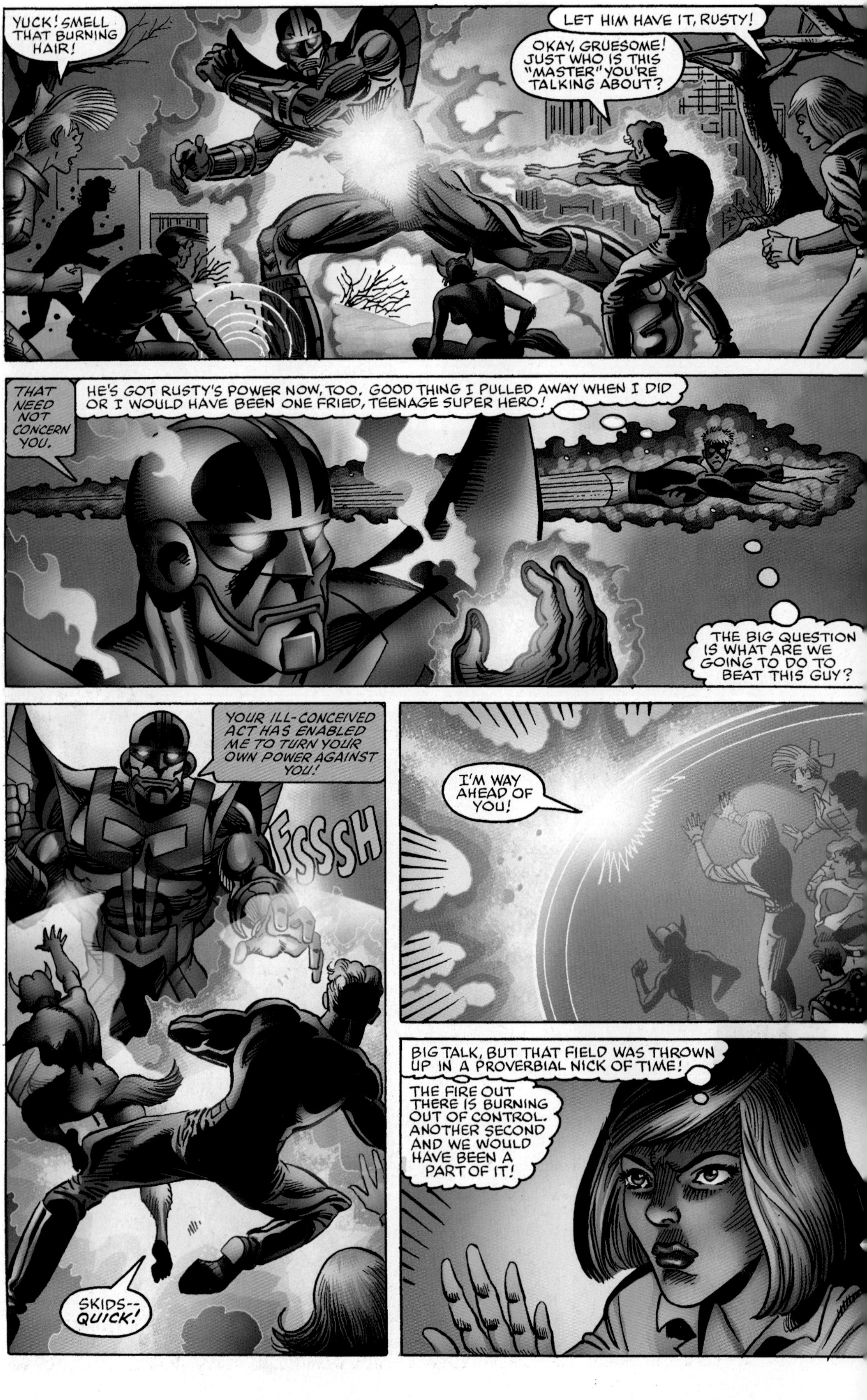
YUCK! SMELL THAT BURNING HAIR!
LET HIM HAVE IT, RUSTY!
OKAY, GRUESOME! JUST WHO IS THIS "MASTER" YOU'RE TALKING ABOUT?
THAT NEED NOT CONCERN YOU.
HE'S GOT RUSTY'S POWER NOW, TOO. GOOD THING I PULLED AWAY WHEN I DID OR I WOULD HAVE BEEN ONE FRIED, TEENAGE SUPER HERO!
THE BIG QUESTION IS WHAT ARE WE GOING TO DO TO BEAT THIS GUY?
YOUR ILL-CONCEIVED ACT HAS ENABLED ME TO TURN YOUR OWN POWER AGAINST YOU!
FSSSH
SKIDS-- QUICK!
I'M WAY AHEAD OF YOU!
BIG TALK, BUT THAT FIELD WAS THROWN UP IN A PROVERBIAL NICK OF TIME!
THE FIRE OUT THERE IS BURNING OUT OF CONTROL. ANOTHER SECOND AND WE WOULD HAVE BEEN A PART OF IT!

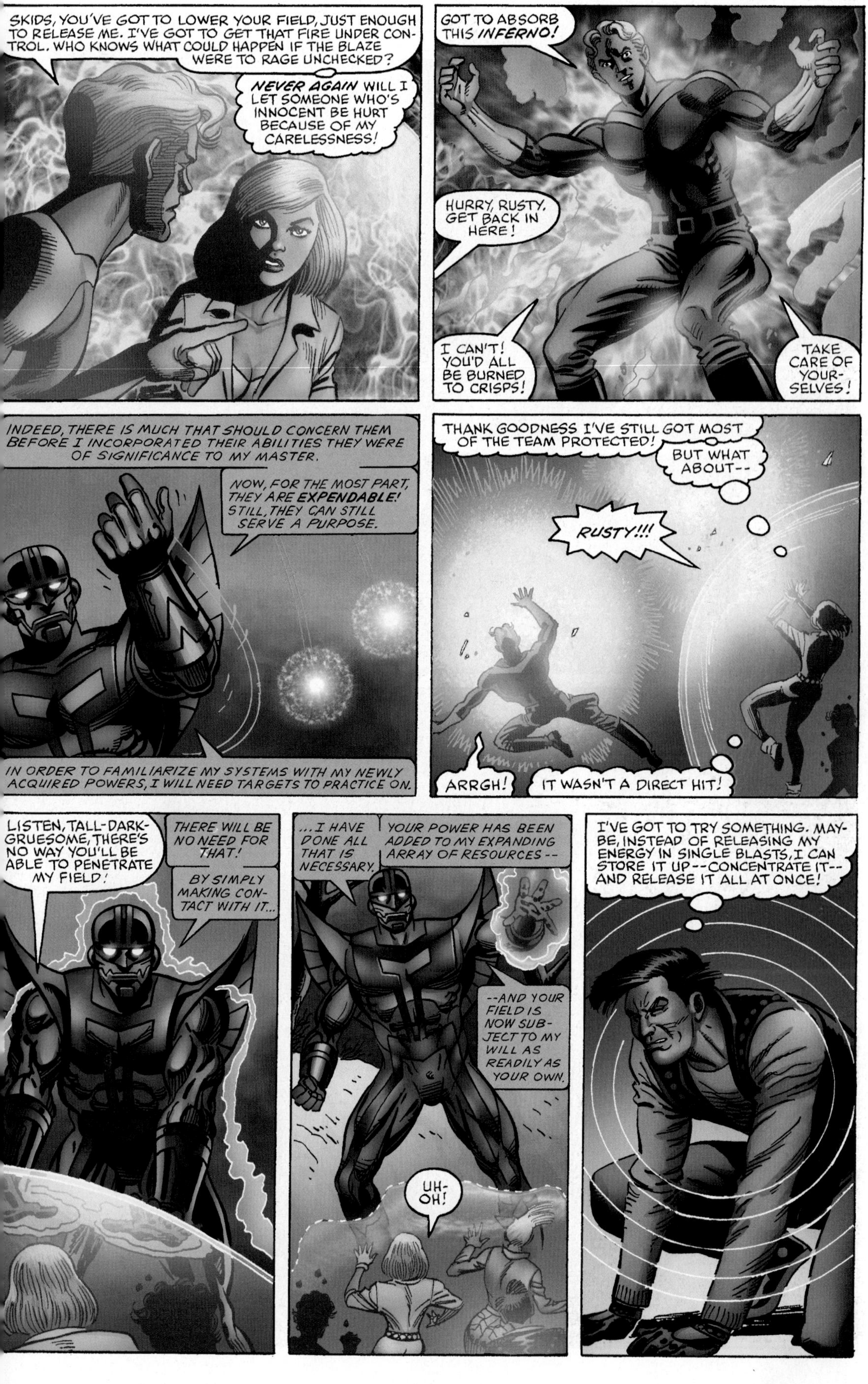
SKIDS, YOU'VE GOT TO LOWER YOUR FIELD, JUST ENOUGH TO RELEASE ME. I'VE GOT TO GET THAT FIRE UNDER CONTROL. WHO KNOWS WHAT COULD HAPPEN IF THE BLAZE WERE TO RAGE UNCHECKED?
NEVER AGAIN WILL I LET SOMEONE WHO'S INNOCENT BE HURT BECAUSE OF MY CARELESSNESS!
GOT TO ABSORB THIS INFERNO!
HURRY, RUSTY. GET BACK IN HERE!
I CAN'T! YOU'D ALL BE BURNED TO CRISPS!
TAKE CARE OF YOURSELVES!
INDEED, THERE IS MUCH THAT SHOULD CONCERN THEM BEFORE I INCORPORATED THEIR ABILITIES THEY WERE OF SIGNIFICANCE TO MY MASTER.
NOW, FOR THE MOST PART, THEY ARE EXPENDABLE! STILL, THEY CAN STILL SERVE A PURPOSE.
IN ORDER TO FAMILIARIZE MY SYSTEMS WITH MY NEWLY ACQUIRED POWERS, I WILL NEED TARGETS TO PRACTICE ON.
THANK GOODNESS I'VE STILL GOT MOST OF THE TEAM PROTECTED!
BUT WHAT ABOUT--
RUSTY!!!
ARRGH!
IT WASN'T A DIRECT HIT!
LISTEN, TALL-DARK-GRUESOME, THERE'S NO WAY YOU'LL BE ABLE TO PENETRATE MY FIELD!
THERE WILL BE NO NEED FOR THAT!
BY SIMPLY MAKING CONTACT WITH IT...
...I HAVE DONE ALL THAT IS NECESSARY.
YOUR POWER HAS BEEN ADDED TO MY EXPANDING ARRAY OF RESOURCES --
--AND YOUR FIELD IS NOW SUBJECT TO MY WILL AS READILY AS YOUR OWN.
UH-OH!
I'VE GOT TO TRY SOMETHING. MAYBE, INSTEAD OF RELEASING MY ENERGY IN SINGLE BLASTS, I CAN STORE IT UP--CONCENTRATE IT--AND RELEASE IT ALL AT ONCE!

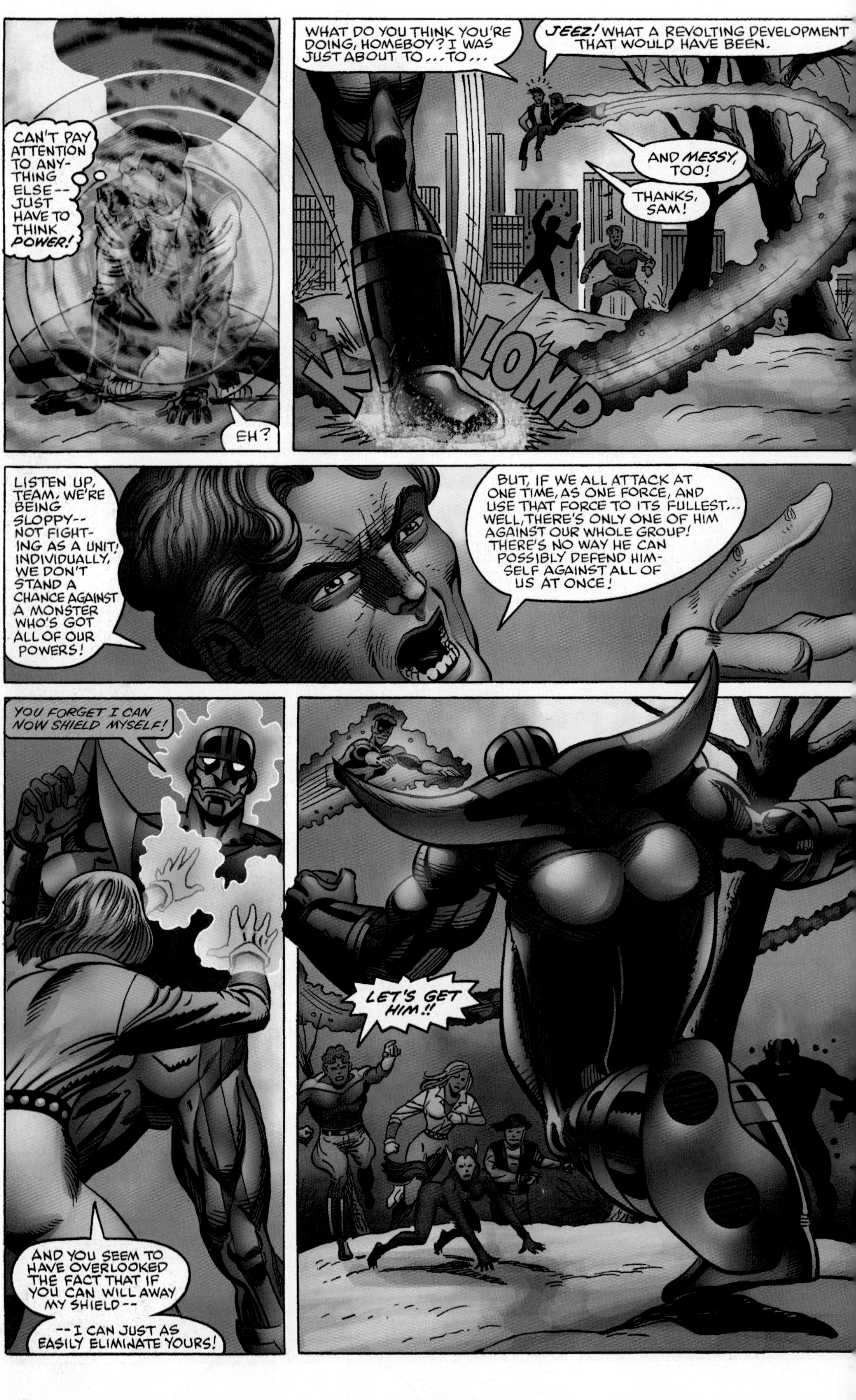
CAN'T PAY ATTENTION TO ANYTHING ELSE-- JUST HAVE TO THINK POWER!
EH?
WHAT DO YOU THINK YOU'RE DOING, HOMEBOY? I WAS JUST ABOUT TO...TO...
JEEZ! WHAT A REVOLTING DEVELOPMENT THAT WOULD HAVE BEEN.
AND MESSY, TOO!
THANKS, SAM!
KLOMP
LISTEN UP, TEAM. WE'RE BEING SLOPPY-- NOT FIGHTING AS A UNIT! INDIVIDUALLY, WE DON'T STAND A CHANCE AGAINST A MONSTER WHO'S GOT ALL OF OUR POWERS!
BUT, IF WE ALL ATTACK AT ONE TIME, AS ONE FORCE, AND USE THAT FORCE TO ITS FULLEST... WELL, THERE'S ONLY ONE OF HIM AGAINST OUR WHOLE GROUP! THERE'S NO WAY HE CAN POSSIBLY DEFEND HIMSELF AGAINST ALL OF US AT ONCE!
YOU FORGET I CAN NOW SHIELD MYSELF!
AND YOU SEEM TO HAVE OVERLOOKED THE FACT THAT IF YOU CAN WILL AWAY MY SHIELD--
--I CAN JUST AS EASILY ELIMINATE YOURS!
LET'S GET HIM!!

SHA

KBRAKT

FSSH

BOOM

KRAK

WEEDWEEO

KEEP IT UP, MUTIES! WE'VE GOT HIM NOW!

HEY, WHAT'S HAPPENING?

HE'S JUST STANDING THERE LIKE SOME SORT OF *GIANT STATUE!*

IT'S LIKE HIS MIND'S BEEN COMPLETELY TURNED OFF!

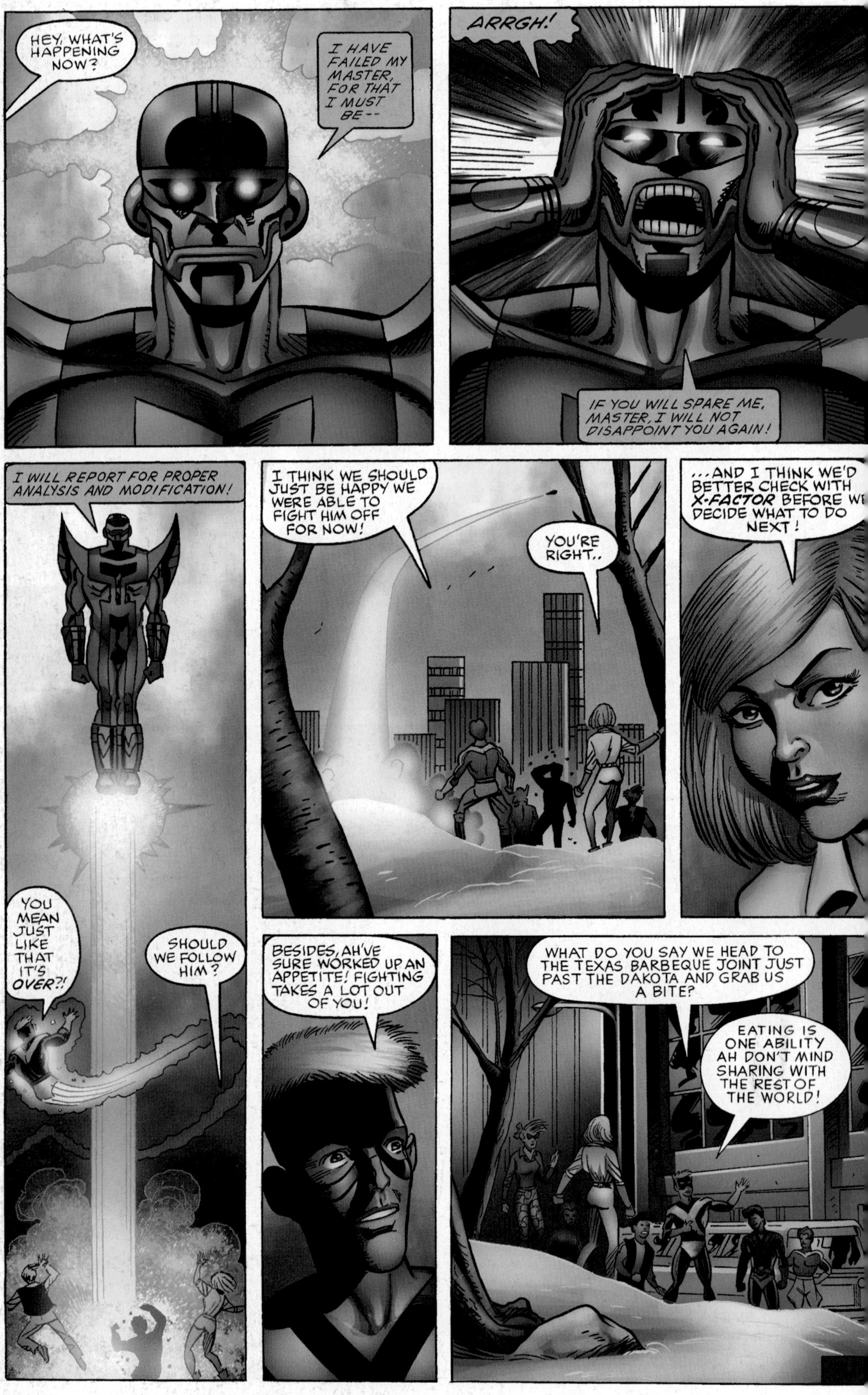
HEY, WHAT'S HAPPENING NOW?
I HAVE FAILED MY MASTER, FOR THAT I MUST BE--
ARRGH!
IF YOU WILL SPARE ME, MASTER, I WILL NOT DISAPPOINT YOU AGAIN!
I WILL REPORT FOR PROPER ANALYSIS AND MODIFICATION!
YOU MEAN JUST LIKE THAT IT'S OVER?!
SHOULD WE FOLLOW HIM?
I THINK WE SHOULD JUST BE HAPPY WE WERE ABLE TO FIGHT HIM OFF FOR NOW!
YOU'RE RIGHT..
...AND I THINK WE'D BETTER CHECK WITH X-FACTOR BEFORE WE DECIDE WHAT TO DO NEXT!
BESIDES, AH'VE SURE WORKED UP AN APPETITE! FIGHTING TAKES A LOT OUT OF YOU!
WHAT DO YOU SAY WE HEAD TO THE TEXAS BARBEQUE JOINT JUST PAST THE DAKOTA AND GRAB US A BITE?
EATING IS ONE ABILITY AH DON'T MIND SHARING WITH THE REST OF THE WORLD!

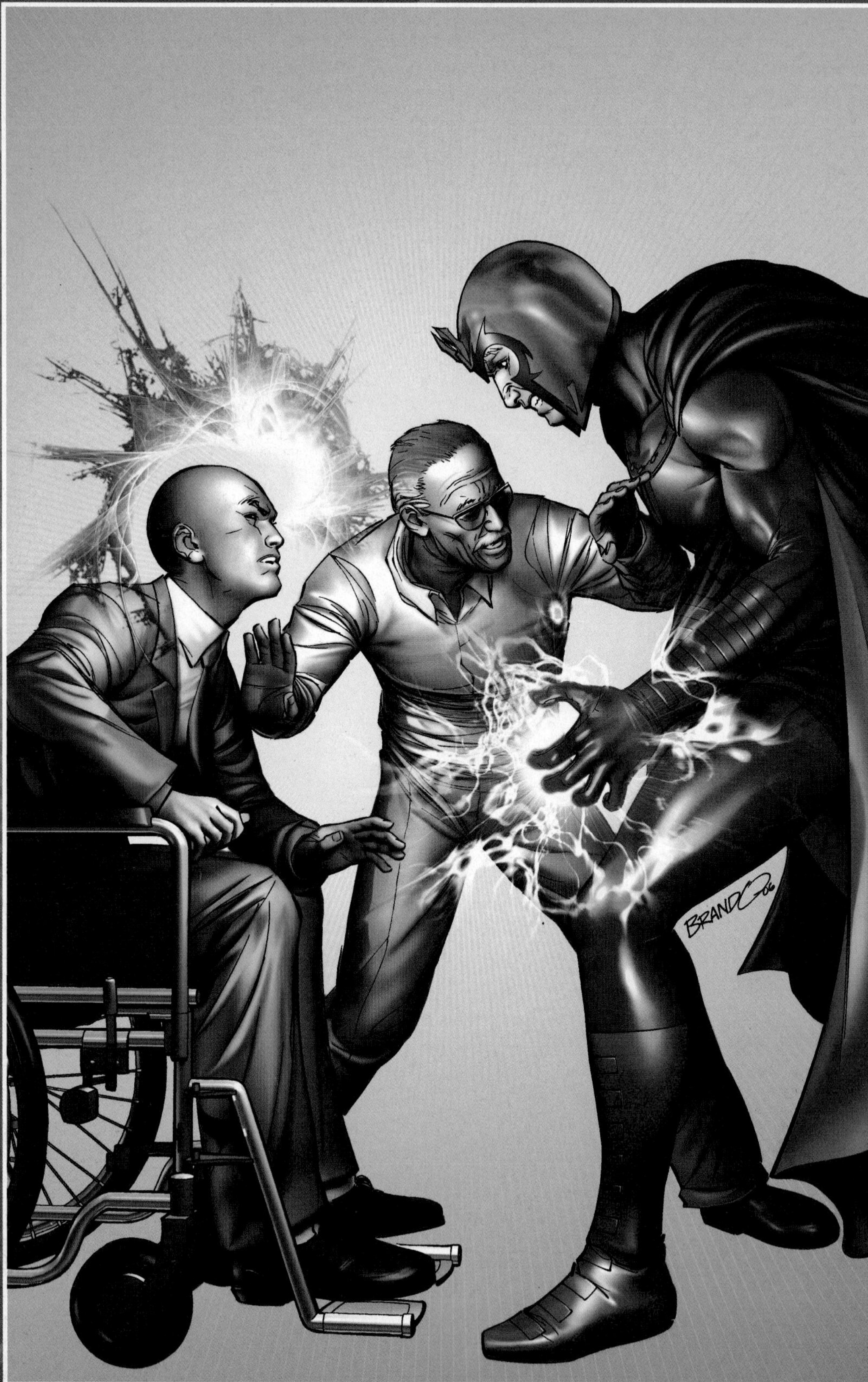

X-MEN: THE UNLIKEY SAGA OF XAVIER, MAGNETO AND STAN

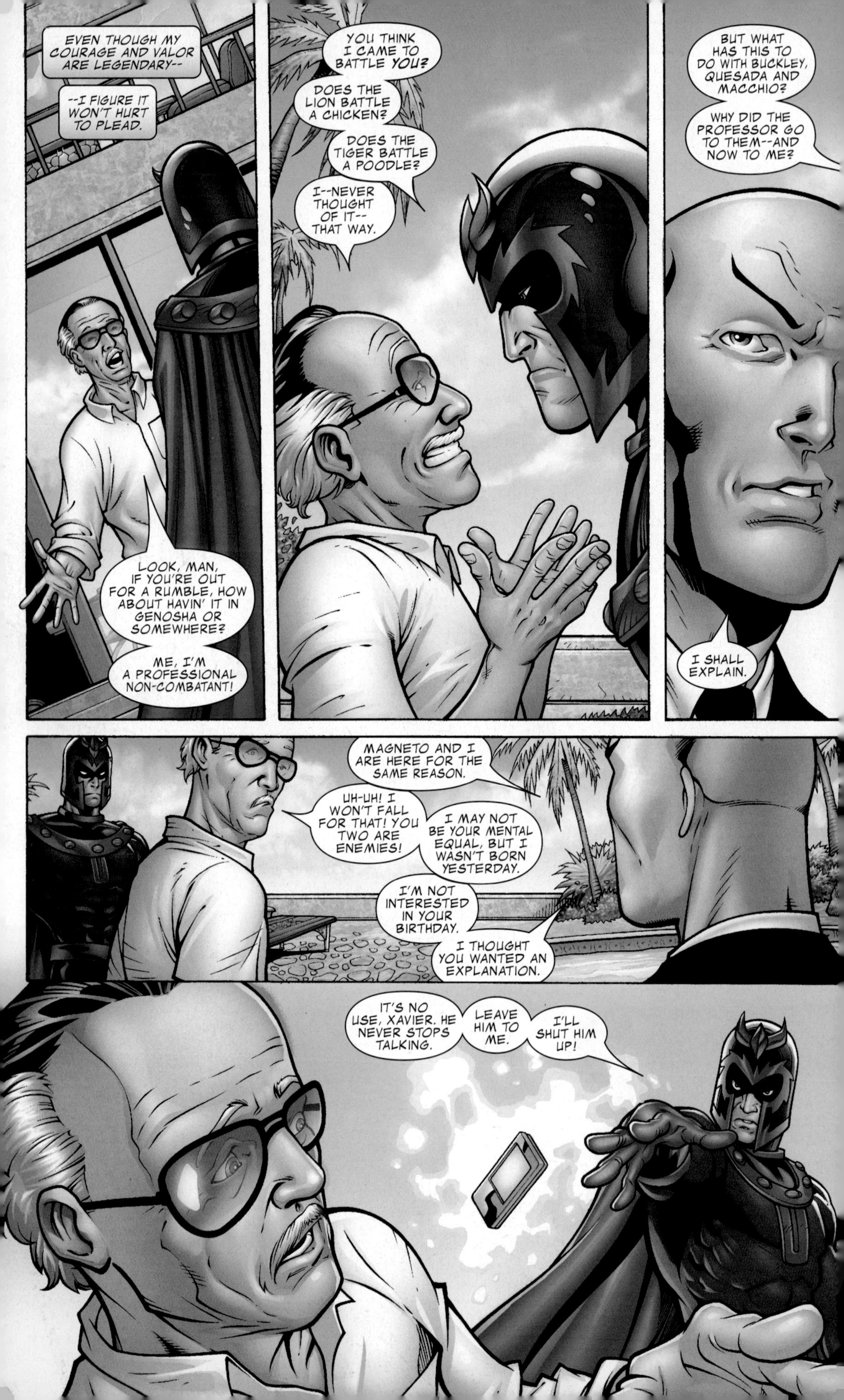
EVEN THOUGH MY COURAGE AND VALOR ARE LEGENDARY--
--I FIGURE IT WON'T HURT TO PLEAD.
LOOK, MAN, IF YOU'RE OUT FOR A RUMBLE, HOW ABOUT HAVIN' IT IN GENOSHA OR SOMEWHERE?
ME, I'M A PROFESSIONAL NON-COMBATANT!
YOU THINK I CAME TO BATTLE YOU?
DOES THE LION BATTLE A CHICKEN?
DOES THE TIGER BATTLE A POODLE?
I--NEVER THOUGHT OF IT--THAT WAY.
BUT WHAT HAS THIS TO DO WITH BUCKLEY, QUESADA AND MACCHIO?
WHY DID THE PROFESSOR GO TO THEM--AND NOW TO ME?
I SHALL EXPLAIN.
MAGNETO AND I ARE HERE FOR THE SAME REASON.
UH-UH! I WON'T FALL FOR THAT! YOU TWO ARE ENEMIES!
I MAY NOT BE YOUR MENTAL EQUAL, BUT I WASN'T BORN YESTERDAY.
I'M NOT INTERESTED IN YOUR BIRTHDAY.
I THOUGHT YOU WANTED AN EXPLANATION.
IT'S NO USE, XAVIER. HE NEVER STOPS TALKING.
LEAVE HIM TO ME.
I'LL SHUT HIM UP!

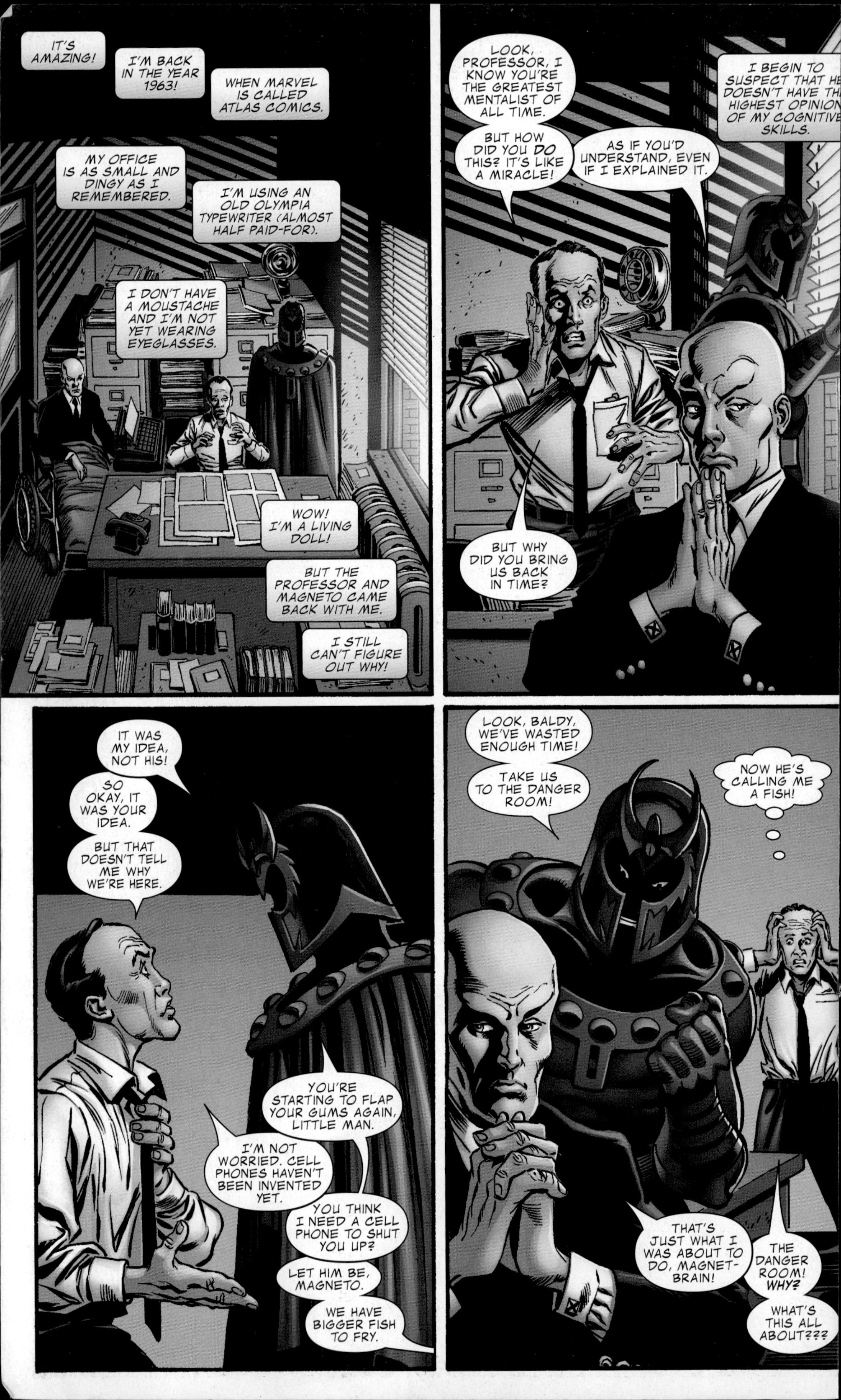
IT'S AMAZING!
I'M BACK IN THE YEAR 1963!
WHEN MARVEL IS CALLED ATLAS COMICS.
MY OFFICE IS AS SMALL AND DINGY AS I REMEMBERED.
I'M USING AN OLD OLYMPIA TYPEWRITER (ALMOST HALF PAID-FOR).
I DON'T HAVE A MOUSTACHE AND I'M NOT YET WEARING EYEGLASSES.
WOW! I'M A LIVING DOLL!
BUT THE PROFESSOR AND MAGNETO CAME BACK WITH ME.
I STILL CAN'T FIGURE OUT WHY!
LOOK, PROFESSOR, I KNOW YOU'RE THE GREATEST MENTALIST OF ALL TIME.
BUT HOW DID YOU DO THIS? IT'S LIKE A MIRACLE!
AS IF YOU'D UNDERSTAND, EVEN IF I EXPLAINED IT.
I BEGIN TO SUSPECT THAT HE DOESN'T HAVE THE HIGHEST OPINION OF MY COGNITIVE SKILLS.
BUT WHY DID YOU BRING US BACK IN TIME?
IT WAS MY IDEA, NOT HIS!
SO OKAY, IT WAS YOUR IDEA.
BUT THAT DOESN'T TELL ME WHY WE'RE HERE.
YOU'RE STARTING TO FLAP YOUR GUMS AGAIN, LITTLE MAN.
I'M NOT WORRIED. CELL PHONES HAVEN'T BEEN INVENTED YET.
YOU THINK I NEED A CELL PHONE TO SHUT YOU UP?
LET HIM BE, MAGNETO.
WE HAVE BIGGER FISH TO FRY.
LOOK, BALDY, WE'VE WASTED ENOUGH TIME!
TAKE US TO THE DANGER ROOM!
NOW HE'S CALLING ME A FISH!
THAT'S JUST WHAT I WAS ABOUT TO DO, MAGNET-BRAIN!
THE DANGER ROOM! WHY?
WHAT'S THIS ALL ABOUT???

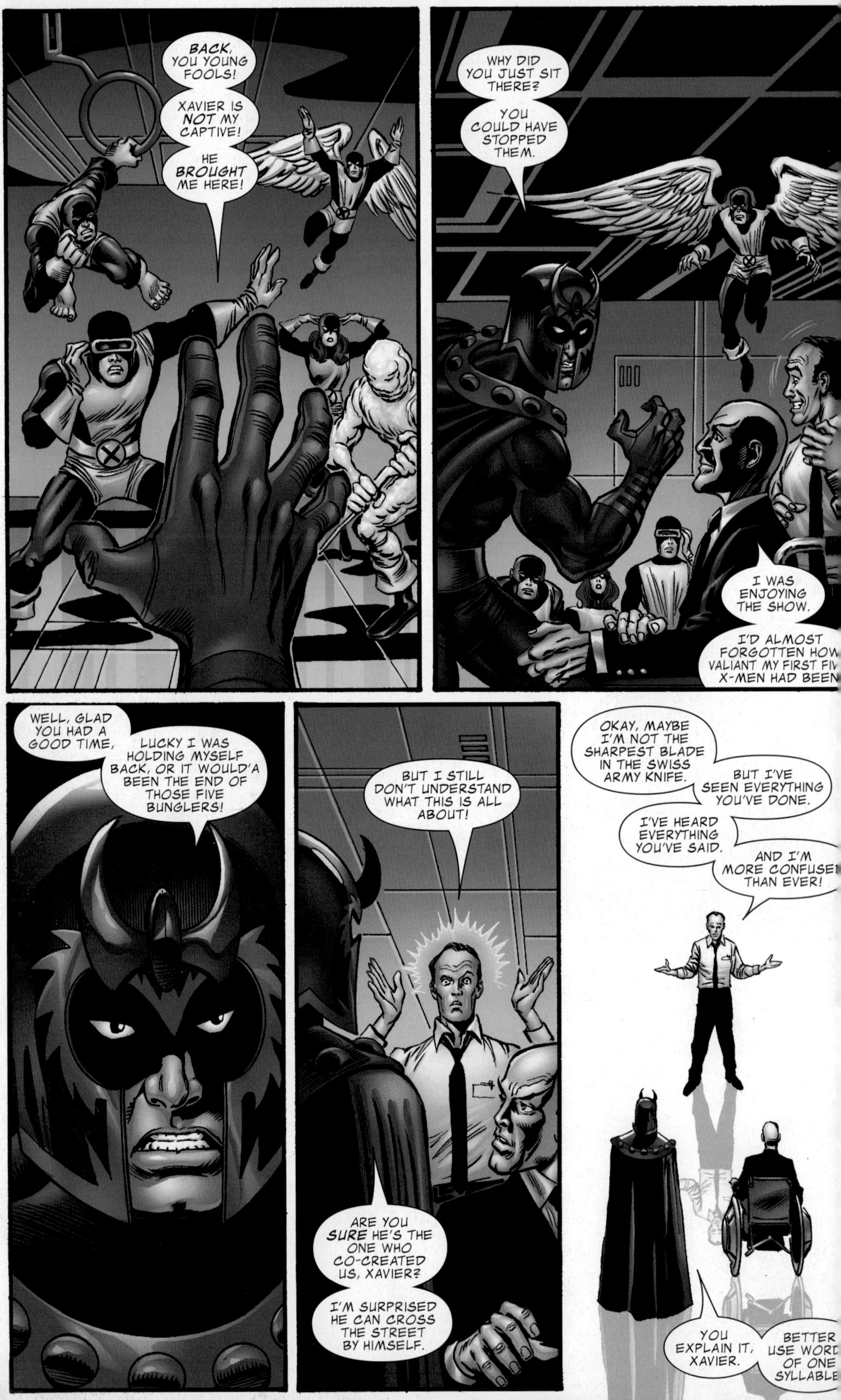

BACK, YOU YOUNG FOOLS!
XAVIER IS NOT MY CAPTIVE!
HE BROUGHT ME HERE!
WHY DID YOU JUST SIT THERE?
YOU COULD HAVE STOPPED THEM.
I WAS ENJOYING THE SHOW.
I'D ALMOST FORGOTTEN HOW VALIANT MY FIRST FIV X-MEN HAD BEEN
WELL, GLAD YOU HAD A GOOD TIME.
LUCKY I WAS HOLDING MYSELF BACK, OR IT WOULD'A BEEN THE END OF THOSE FIVE BUNGLERS!
BUT I STILL DON'T UNDERSTAND WHAT THIS IS ALL ABOUT!
ARE YOU SURE HE'S THE ONE WHO CO-CREATED US, XAVIER?
I'M SURPRISED HE CAN CROSS THE STREET BY HIMSELF.
OKAY, MAYBE I'M NOT THE SHARPEST BLADE IN THE SWISS ARMY KNIFE.
BUT I'VE SEEN EVERYTHING YOU'VE DONE.
I'VE HEARD EVERYTHING YOU'VE SAID.
AND I'M MORE CONFUSE THAN EVER!
YOU EXPLAIN IT, XAVIER.
BETTER USE WORD OF ONE SYLLABLE

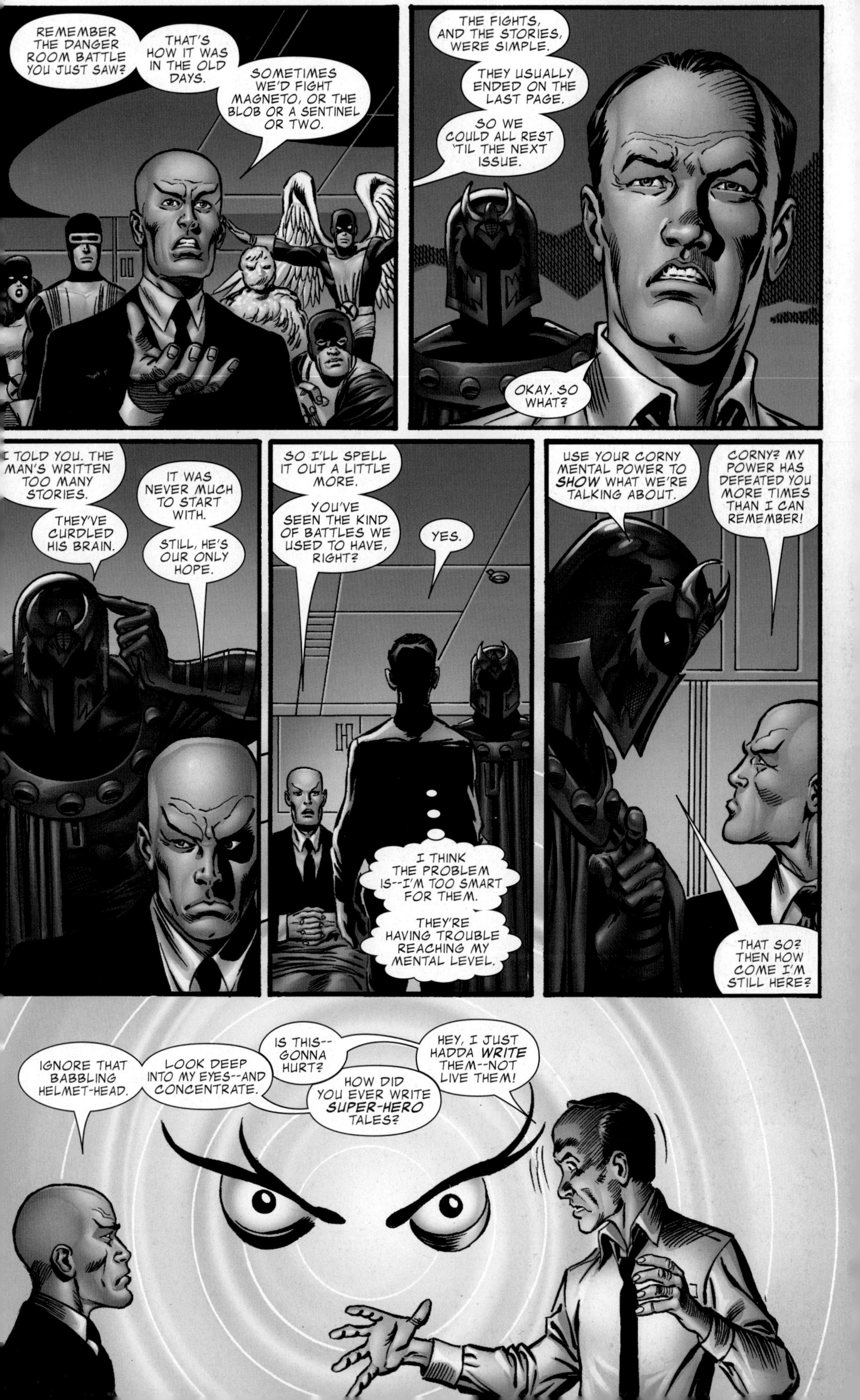
REMEMBER THE DANGER ROOM BATTLE YOU JUST SAW?
THAT'S HOW IT WAS IN THE OLD DAYS.
SOMETIMES WE'D FIGHT MAGNETO, OR THE BLOB OR A SENTINEL OR TWO.
THE FIGHTS, AND THE STORIES, WERE SIMPLE.
THEY USUALLY ENDED ON THE LAST PAGE.
SO WE COULD ALL REST 'TIL THE NEXT ISSUE.
OKAY. SO WHAT?
I TOLD YOU. THE MAN'S WRITTEN TOO MANY STORIES.
THEY'VE CURDLED HIS BRAIN.
IT WAS NEVER MUCH TO START WITH.
STILL, HE'S OUR ONLY HOPE.
SO I'LL SPELL IT OUT A LITTLE MORE.
YOU'VE SEEN THE KIND OF BATTLES WE USED TO HAVE, RIGHT?
YES.
I THINK THE PROBLEM IS--I'M TOO SMART FOR THEM.
THEY'RE HAVING TROUBLE REACHING MY MENTAL LEVEL.
USE YOUR CORNY MENTAL POWER TO SHOW WHAT WE'RE TALKING ABOUT.
CORNY? MY POWER HAS DEFEATED YOU MORE TIMES THAN I CAN REMEMBER!
THAT SO? THEN HOW COME I'M STILL HERE?
IGNORE THAT BABBLING HELMET-HEAD.
LOOK DEEP INTO MY EYES--AND CONCENTRATE.
IS THIS--GONNA HURT?
HOW DID YOU EVER WRITE SUPER-HERO TALES?
HEY, I JUST HADDA WRITE THEM--NOT LIVE THEM!

THE UNLIKELY SAGA OF

XAVIER, MAGNETO AND STAN

WRITTEN BY: **STAN LEE**

DRAWN BY: RON LIM (INKS: MOSTAFA MOUSSA) PAGES 1, 4-5 & 22 | BEN OLIVER PAGES 2-3 | RON FRENZ (INKS: TOM PALMER) PAGES 6-7, 10-11 & 20

KLAUS JANSON PAGES 8-9 | SEAN CHEN (INKS: SANDU FLOREA) PAGES 12-13 | JOHN ROMITA, JR. (INKS: SCOTT HANNA) PAGES 14-15 | PASQUAL FERRY PAGES 16-17 | LEINIL FRANCIS YU PAGES 18-19 | HOWARD CHAYKIN PAGE 21 | BRANDON PETERSON COVER

COLORED BY GURU EFX | LETTERED BY VC'S JOE CARAMAGNA | ASSOCIATE EDITORS JOHN BARBER & NICOLE BOOSE | EDITOR RALPH MACCHIO | EDITOR IN CHIEF JOE QUESADA | PUBLISHER DAN BUCKLEY